Latino Workers
in the Contemporary South

Latino Workers
in the Contemporary South

Edited by Arthur D. Murphy,
Colleen Blanchard, and Jennifer A. Hill

Southern Anthropological Society Proceedings, No. 34

Michael V. Angrosino, Series Editor

The University of Georgia Press

Athens and London

Southern Anthropological Society

Founded 1966

Published by the University of Georgia Press
Athens, Georgia 30602
© 2001 by the Southern Anthropological Society
All rights reserved
Set in 11/13 Times Roman
Printed and bound by Thomson-Shore
The paper in this book meets the guidelines for
permanence and durability of the Committee on
Production Guidelines for Book Longevity of the
Council on Library Resources.

Printed in the United States of America
05 04 03 02 01   C   5   4   3   2   1
05 04 03 02 01   P   5   4   3   2   1

Library of Congress Cataloging-in-Publication Data
Latino workers in the contemporary South / edited by
Arthur D. Murphy, Colleen Blanchard, and Jennifer A. Hill
p. cm. — (Southern Anthropological Society proceedings ; no. 34)
Includes bibliographical references.
ISBN 0-8203-2278-4 (alk. paper)—ISBN 0-8203-2279-2 (pbk. : alk. paper)
1. Hispanic Americans—Employment—Southern States.
2. Mexican Americans—Employment—Southern States.
3. Alien labor, Mexican—Employment—Southern States.
4. Southern States—Emigration and immigration.
5. Southern States—Social conditions. 6. Southern States—Race relations.
I. Murphy, Arthur D. II. Blanchard, Colleen. III. Hill, Jennifer A. IV. Series
HD8081.H7 L375 2001
305.868'075—dc21   00-045135

British Library Cataloging-in-Publication Data available

Contents

Latino Workers
in the Contemporary South

Introduction: From *Patrones* and *Caciques* to Good Ole Boys

Deborah A. Duchon and Arthur D. Murphy

In the late 1980s and early 1990s, citizens of the southern United States awoke to the realization that their cities and counties no longer consisted of residents who could be divided along the traditional racial or ethnic lines of black and white (Dameron and Murphy 1997; Duchon 1993; Fennell 1977; Hill 1979; Murphy 1997). Many major cities, such as Atlanta, Mobile, Charlotte, and Greenville, hosted large numbers of Southeast Asian, European, African, and Latin American immigrants. The largest single group among the new immigrants is Mexican. Mostly undocumented, Mexican immigrants have transformed the face of much of the region, a trend seen not only in large cities. Smaller localities, particularly those that host industries requiring many low-wage workers (Griffith and Kissam 1994; Lamphere, Stepick, and Grenier 1994; Stull, Broadway, and Griffith 1995), suddenly found themselves having to deal with schoolchildren who did not speak English and parents who did not understand the legal and social systems of the United States.

One of the major reasons for this influx of refugees and immigrants to the South was the strong economic growth experienced by the region. Between 1977 and 1992, the economy of the South outperformed all other regions of the country, as well as the aggregate national economy. The strong economic performance of the South at a time when the nation was under increasing pressure to admit refugees from Southeast Asia, the former Soviet Union, Eastern Europe, and Africa led the State Department to choose the region as a target area in which to settle refugees who were not being sponsored by family members in other parts of the country. Mexican immigration is likewise characterized by a growing economy dependent on abundant, inexpensive labor and a population willing to fill such positions.

The essays in this volume are an attempt to explain and describe the new immigrants to the South. While our focus is on Mexicans, much of what they have experienced can be generalized to all new immigrant and refugee populations in the region. One would probably expect such populations to have a hard time in the South, and indeed in some cases at the beginning of the new phase of immigration service providers were concerned for the very lives of the new residents (Viviano 1986). After all, the South has a history of racial intolerance, xenophobia, and poverty. Quite the opposite, however, has been true in the long run. After some difficult early years during which Mexicans, Asians, and other immigrants were subjected to racial and ethnic intolerance, the traditional ethnic groups (white and black) of the region have begun to appreciate and value the contributions newcomers have made. We cannot fully explain why this has been the case, but our investigations of the process have taught us a great deal about how resettlement and assimilation assistance was managed in much of the region. The essays in this volume report on how Mexicans have fared as they settle in the South.

POLICY AND PRACTICE

Congress sets federal policy based on humanitarian, diplomatic, political, and economic considerations, factors that are both overlapping and often in conflict with one another. Documents released by the State Department stress the importance of humanitarian concerns to the psychology of refugee and new immigrant resettlement. These statements link the refugee program to the country as a whole, a nation of immigrants, a place where the "wretched refuse," so to speak, can come to get a new start. There is also a sense of fair play and the importance of charity and doing right by those who have stood by us in times of conflict. The rhetoric of refugee and immigration policy is full of the language of humanitarian concern.

The Refugee Act of 1980, which serves as the basis of the Refugee Resettlement Program, was written partly as a result of international pressure for the United States to accept the same definition of *refugee* as the United Nations. Until that time, U.S. refugee policy was largely tied to the cold war, with preference for the resettlement of people from the Soviet bloc, Cuba, and (starting in the mid-1970s) Southeast Asia. Even today, federal reports stress that the United States accepts more new residents each year for permanent resettlement than all other nations in the world combined.

Immigration of any sort is a highly political issue. In some parts of the United States, immigrants are highly desired because of their contributions to the labor force and economy. In other areas, where the economic needs are less pressing, there is a corresponding lack of enthusiasm for the acceptance of newcomers. For that reason, states may or may not elect to participate in federal programs such as refugee resettlement.

Federal policy aims to resettle refugees in the most cost-effective ways possible. In other words, the goal of the program is to see to it that the more than 100,000 legally admitted immigrants and refugees each year are not an economic burden to the society. It is fair to say that this is the only tangible consideration when policymakers deal with any immigration issue in the United States, whether it concerns refugees, immigrants, or undocumented workers. Federal policy must therefore balance humanitarianism (and the need for us to maintain our presumed role as the benign leader of the New World Order) with domestic considerations such as politics, jobs, welfare, and the burdens placed on the ordinary taxpayer. The answer has been to commodify refugees and immigrants, to hire contractors to remake them into citizens and taxpayers, and to return guest workers who for some reason or another are found to be defective. People who are sick should be made healthy enough to work, and English-language training is given top priority because it is seen as the key to employment. Entrants must become economically self-sufficient as soon as possible.

As a result of the emphasis on self-sufficiency and the use of outside contractors, a substantial amount of federal money flows into states that participate in federal programs such as the Refugee Resettlement Program and others designed to lessen the negative economic impact newcomers might have on a region. In the case of refugees, the Office of Refugee Resettlement guides the structure of refugee resettlement at the state level. Funds are under the jurisdiction of the state human services department, and there are to be state-level refugee coordinators and a state refugee health coordinator. Funds are to be used primarily for employment services, English-language training, and social adjustments as determined by each state. There is to be a board advising the state refugee coordinator, composed of state contractors and

other local experts and activists. Within that structure there is wide lati-
tude for the state to set up its own structure and use the funding as
necessary to meet local conditions. As a result, the states vary greatly
in their programs, reflecting the culture of the state. One of the greatest variations is in how refugees and other immigrants are viewed by
the state structure. Are they a single group to be supported in their efforts to settle in the state, or are they distinct populations balkanized
by separate pots of money and distinct immigration status?

The latter is true of Georgia. Net migration to the state is about
100,000 per year, including refugees, immigrants, and, most important,
Americans moving from other states, mainly for jobs, but also to retire
and enjoy the mild climate and relatively low cost of living. Like other
southern states, Georgia is a mass of contradictions. It has one of the
fastest-expanding economies in the country, with one of the lowest unemployment rates. Overall personal income is in the upper half of all
states, yet 26 percent of its residents live at or below the poverty level.
Georgia boasts world-class medical facilities yet ranks in the lowest
quintile in infant deaths and births to teenage mothers (Akioka 1998).
More than one hundred languages are spoken within its borders, yet
many school systems lack ESL programs, and the state school superin-
tendent is hostile to expanding such programs.

Despite the growth and modernization in the New South in the past
thirty years, things in Georgia, as in other states in the region, are still
done much as they always have been. State government is still run by
the same officials who have held elective office for years and years. @
good-ole-boy system prevails, an informal network driven by unequal
and reciprocal personal relationships. The system usually revolves
around one strong man who picks his cohorts and accessories. For instance, the most powerful man in state government, and the biggest good
ole boy in the state, is, in most cases, the Speaker of the House. He not
only decides who holds important committee chairs but also controls
the flow of legislation and the nominations from his party for statewide
office, including those for governor and U.S. senator. Any governor who
wants to pass legislation must get the Speaker's blessing before he will
guarantee its passage.

Because the good-ole-boy network is based on personal relationships,
it superficially appears to be relaxed and accessible. In fact, it is difficult

to become part of a system that is based on years of personal contacts, as opposed to more objectified results-oriented standards. As a result, members of the network get priority year after year, while the ideas and actions of newcomers are resisted, albeit politely. It also means that ineffectiveness, even misbehavior, on the part of good ole boys may be tolerated, because personal relationships take precedence over measurable accomplishments—or lack thereof. The other side of the coin is that persons excluded from the network receive harsh punishment for misdeeds so as to keep up the appearance of self-policing. In one recent case, a group of lobbyists sent members of the state legislature's good-ole-boy network on a weekend golfing holiday, accompanied by two women from a local strip club. When the story broke in the local press, insiders responded as if the crime was being caught. Forced by the media to take action, the legislature punished the offenders with a mild slap on the wrist. A few months later, a young African American legislator, not a member of the network and indeed known to cause the good ole boys difficulties from time to time, was caught returning from a vacation trip with a minuscule amount of marijuana in his possession. He was almost impeached by a legislature incensed over the immorality of his conduct and the bad example it would set for the children of the state.

The same model holds true for most refugee and immigrant programs in the region. The central figure is the refugee coordinator, whose job is to oversee funding from the Office of Refugee Resettlement; in many cases the coordinator also sets policy for other immigrant programs. In one example, the coordinator is a good ole boy with a doctorate. He is a caring individual, liked by one and all. He considers himself to be an innovator, and early in his career he worked as a community organizer. In fact, he has been willing to take more chances in programming than his predecessors. Southerner that he is, however, civility is his top priority. When asked why refugees seem to adapt so well to the South, he does not mention the economy and availability of jobs, but instead replied, "Well, Southerners are just naturally hospitable. Refugees from a lot of the countries just tend to be more modest, and I think that's appreciated." He continued, referring to the Russians (who, to many Americans, seem pushy and insensitive) as an example of an immigrant group that might be better suited to life in the North. He takes great pride in the fact that all the agencies he funds treat each other (and the other agencies with which they have to work) with greater civility than is found in most other states. And they do—superficially.

Like any other southern politician (and let there be no doubt that a state's refugee or immigrant coordinator is a political position), this coordinator surrounds himself with his own set of good ole boys. Not all of them are male, but all of them are people he is most comfortable with. This group is composed mainly of refugees, immigrants, and others who tend to come from elite families in their home countries and who have resided in the United States for more than twenty years. They know they can count on the coordinator to divert a large portion of his funds their way while providing other agencies with minimal funding. For example, during the 1990–95 period, the last for which data are available, 50 percent of the state's refugee funds went to just four agencies. The remainder was divided among at least thirty other service providers.

As in any good-ole-boy system, misbehavior is tolerated in exchange for loyalty. For instance, one of the service providers owned a doughnut shop near the agency he headed. His wife was the manager of the business. He would check messages at his office every morning and then go to the doughnut shop for the rest of the day. It was an open secret. When a woman community activist of the same ethnicity complained to the state office, she was told that it was okay because it was done all the time in the man's country of origin. She was outraged. In the first place, she explained, even if officials in the home country tolerated this type of corruption, it did not make it right. It was not an issue of cultural relativity. Nothing was done, and so she went to a reporter, who accompanied her to the doughnut shop and then called the state to investigate. He received the same answer—that it was culturally appropriate behavior and therefore okay. When the reporter threatened to go public with the story, complete with photos, the state coordinator put a stop to the practice. The shop was sold, but the agency and its head were not punished. But, as in the case of the young black legislator mentioned earlier, an example had to be made, so a caseworker was fired for improperly charging his clients $15 a head for services.

In another instance, the head of a different agency (himself an immigrant) arranged to place incoming clients in an apartment complex in a dangerous neighborhood far from any service locations. The complex had recently been purchased by a group of immigrant investors, and the open assumption by all members of the community was that the director was receiving a kickback from the owners. To date, no investigation has taken place. It should be noted that the errant agencies in these two cases were among the four that had received the bulk of the state's refugee funding. In these and other cases, those who have complained to the state have had their funding either cut or suspended in the following funding cycle. In some cases, they have also been moved out of the loop by being taken off the advisory council.

An additional problem with this system is that it flies in the face of federal policy, which sets a five-year limit on refugee status and encourages immigrant self-sufficiency. The idea is to keep the flow going, to keep immigrants and refugees moving into the mainstream. As one group moves into the mainstream, its caseworkers should be replaced by workers from newer immigrant and refugee streams. This turnover, however, does not happen. Once an individual is part of the system that provides services to refugees and becomes part of the good-ole-boy network, he or she can expect employment for life. The route to self-improvement for many early immigrants, who learned the system by working as caseworkers, is thereby denied to later arrivals.

This system also runs counter to the stated policy that services should be provided by culturally appropriate caseworkers. New immigrants and refugees are often of different ethnicity from those who serve them, even if North Americans tend to lump them all together. So, in other good-ole-boy agencies, the problem is explained away by saying, "Well, after all, they are all Muslims and speak Arabic as a common language," or, "They are all Latinos and speak Spanish, don't they?" The problem is that although Arabic has a common written language, the spoken language varies widely. Immigrants from Mexico and Central America are intimidated by what they see as a superiority complex on the part of Cuban and Puerto Rican providers who, because of their legal status, are the primary source of Spanish-speaking caseworkers for social service agencies and schools. The policy itself ignores the fact that many immigrants and refugees prefer receiving services from bilingual Anglo or African Americans because they do not wish to become involved in a re-creation of the old system of political strong men, the *caciques* and *patrones* they left in the old country. It is not that immigrants and refugees are "naturally" polite, or that they share strong family values and so fit into southern culture. Rather, their assimilation may be due to the fact that they come from a good-ole-boy system and know how it works. The problem for them and for the rest of the South will come not from the immigrants but from those moving from other parts of the United States, who demand a more open and rational system of distribution of goods and services. In one state, the coordinator retired and was replaced by a much more bureaucratic, objective, and "to the letter" individual. The new person made it clear that no agency could expect funding on an ongoing basis. Each year now brings a new contract with objective peer review. There is a new spirit of efficiency and accountability.

THIS VOLUME

The essays in this volume document the efforts of Mexican immigrants in the South as they try to work their way through this new but strangely familiar system. In many cases, they have attempted to build new organizations meeting their specific needs. Because in many cases they are not part of the good-ole-boy system, however, they find the state attempting to fold them into the models developed for previous groups who have established themselves as "good" immigrants. We have chosen to focus on Latinos and Mexicans because they are, by far, the single largest group in the region. In Georgia, for example, there are estimated to be more Mexicans than all other groups combined, and the ratio tilts even further in their favor during the harvest of Vidalia onions and other high-value crops in the rural central and southern parts of the state. The Mexican migrant workers are so important to this crop that when the Immigration and Naturalization Service (INS) raided the fields, Georgia's senior senator flew down from Washington to arrange a truce between growers and INS to make it possible for the harvest to be completed.

Together, the essays present an overview of the variety of issues immigrants and refugees face as they move into the New South, even as the region itself becomes part of the global economy of the twenty-first century.

REFERENCES

Akioka, L., ed. 1998. *Georgia Statistical Abstract*. Athens: Selig Center for Economic Growth, University of Georgia.

Dameron, R., and A. Murphy. 1997. An International City Too Busy to Hate? Social and Cultural Change in Atlanta, 1970–1995. *Urban Anthropology* 26:43–69.

Duchon, D. 1993. Home Is Where You Make It: Hmong Refugees in Georgia. M.A. thesis, Georgia State University.

Fennell, V. 1977. International Atlanta and Ethnic Group Relations. *Urban Anthropology* 6:345–54.

Griffith, D., and E. Kissam. 1994. *Working Poor: Farmworkers in the United States*. Philadelphia: Temple University Press.

Hill, C. 1979. Toward Internationalism: Urban Continuity and Change in a Southern City. In *Cities in a Larger Context*, ed. T. Collins, 53–57. Athens: University of Georgia Press.

Lamphere, L., A. Stepick, and G. Grenier, eds. 1994. *Newcomers in the Workplace: Immigrants and the Restructuring of the U.S. Economy*. Philadelphia: Temple University Press.

Murphy, A. 1997. Atlanta: Capital of the 21st Century? *Urban Anthropology* 26:1–8.

Stull, D., M. Broadway, and D. Griffith. 1995. *Any Way You Cut It: Meat Processing and Small-Town America*. Lawrence: University Press of Kansas.

Viviano, F. 1986. From the Asian Hills to a U.S. Valley. *Far Eastern Economic Review* 16 (October):47–49.

Ethnicity: Consciousness, Agency, and Status in the World System

Kathryn A. Kozaitis

Contemporary anthropological inquiry into the nature of social and cultural units stresses three factors: the world system and its attendant global political and economic interdependence; the nation-state, which is the normative type of political organization; and the local collectivity as a component of complex societies. Relations among these units of analysis inform and enhance our theoretical understanding of ethnic groups, ethnicity, and interethnic relations. This perspective is especially illuminating when analysis focuses on what people actually do and on the local experience of an ethnic group that operates within a historical context and temporal structural and ideational variables that influence collective consciousness, social reproduction, and political status in the contemporary world (Kozaitis 1993).

Ethnicity is a complicated, volatile, and multifaceted variable. Like race, society, and culture, it is a phenomenon whose understanding rests on a multidimensional, empirical research design and a theoretical perspective that relies on comparison and contrast of historical, structural, and symbolic dimensions of case studies. Anthropological research since World War II has resulted in a number of theories of ethnicity that reflect particular ethnographic sites, bodies of data, and topical foci (Glazer and Moynihan 1976; Thompson 1989).

Given the great variety of self-identified ethnic groups all over the world, can we assume that an effort toward universalism is futile? Can a grand theory of ethnicity help us understand better the plight and experience of particular ethnic groups? To be sure, the case study, supported by empirical data generated by fieldwork within a historical and geopolitical context, is a prerequisite to a more general understanding of ethnic groups. A critical reading of the literature, however, yields a plausible, overriding theoretical framework for understanding ethnicity as a form of sociocultural organization in late modernity (Kottak and Kozaitis 1999; Kozaitis 1997). Critical to an appreciation of ethnicity as a topic of anthropological analysis are theories of sociocultural construction and change.

Knowledge about society and culture owes much to world-system theory, which emphasizes the effects of such large-scale forces as wars, the formation of the nation-state, international trade, capitalism, and colonialism upon local communities and regions (Wallerstein 1979). Contributions by political economists elaborate on and enrich this insight; these scholars shed light on the relations between global forces and local experience by placing the subjects of their research in the midst of historical transformations and global systems of exchange between unequal parties (Roseberry 1988; Wolf 1982). Their approach incorporates history and views local communities as products of international interests in the domain of not only economic power but political domination as well (Wolf 1982). As Wolf observes, "Human populations construct their cultures in interaction with one another, and not in isolation" (1982:ix). Such a "totality of interconnected processes" produces subject groups whose very "formation, construction, and reproduction" are accounted for chiefly by their participation in and relations with a larger social system; they are rooted in a definite historical period (3).

Another perspective on sociocultural units also emphasizes the intersection and interdependency of external forces and internal dynamics. Culture remains as lived experience and as a set of relationships within a political and economic order of domination, not a closed system of construction and reconstruction (R. Williams 1982). This theoretical framework is, however, concerned with internal dynamics of culture and with local agents as active reproducers of culture (Ortner 1984). The proactive role of human actors in this process of making and changing culture is recognized to be of causal significance equal to that of larger forces and systems with which groups come into contact. Although clearly of Weberian descent, the theory of "practice" acknowledges the influence of forces associated with Marxism on human activity; however, it very definitely emphasizes a kind of feedback system of relations and interdependencies between history, structure, and people. As Ortner points out, practice, while emerging from structure, nonetheless reproduces and has the capacity to transform structure.

The view that cultural modes are products of relations and conflicts between unequal systems of power is integral to this strategy. These interactions and contributions by all the forces that participate in this practice in turn reproduce exploitative ideologies, social hierarchies, political asymmetries, and hegemonic relationships. Cultural reproduction and transformation are processes of political struggles between sociocultural entities under circumstances that require cultural contact with outside agents of power (Bourdieu 1977). The qualitative and distinguishing dimension of this approach remains human agency, understood as local forms of interpretation, reception, and resistance.

A more recent anthropological political economy also explains culture as production, a property of human activity, not simply as a product removed from its own process of creation (Roseberry 1988). This school of thought informs us that culture is simultaneously a product of past and present activity and part of the context in which human meaning and behavior exist (Roseberry 1989). Cultural units, be they societies, microregions, or ethnic groups within host nation-states, are contextualized within the historical process from which they came to be and the structures of power that channel their reproduction. Although this framework places the local group at the center of analysis, as does practice theory, it is resolutely deterministic in its emphasis; it contends that both human activity and meaning are necessarily shaped by inequality and domination imposed by external forces on internal order.

The anthropological study of sociocultural units as isolated, self-sustained, and independent of a larger system is not viable when the subject group in question is itself a subject collectivity that must exist and reproduce itself within a larger social system. All social and cultural units are part of a "global ethnoscape" (Appadurai 1991), entities whose identity, status, and change cannot be understood apart from history and the place they hold in national and international hierarchies of political power, economic well-being, and "symbolic capital" (Bourdieu 1977; Roseberry 1989). The historical events and structures of power that shape and constrain local activity are integral factors of contemporary analysis and interpretation. Equally significant is the nature of organized life and the voice and work of human beings who constitute a sociocultural unit. The constructivist theories of society and culture outlined above enrich our understanding of ethnicity as a key variable and the ethnic group as a unit of anthropological research and analysis.

ETHNICITY AS AN ANTHROPOLOGICAL VARIABLE

Four decades ago, Wagley and Harris (1958) demonstrated that an anthropological view of minority groups is intrinsically synchronic, diachronic, and comparative. Consideration of the following four principles guided their conceptual paradigm: long-term processes of sociocultural evolution; the "pre-minority past," that is, the historical heritage of a group and the conditions that brought about its genesis as a subordinate collectivity in a host society; the "functional relations" between the minority group and the dominant social order; and the group's similarities to and differences from analogous cultural units and social arrangements during comparable epochs (1958:237–96). Recognition and acknowledgement of historical, political, economic, and sociological factors, including such conditions as technological change, wars, revolutions, and global trends, inform their approach.

According to Wagley and Harris, past and present contexts and structural relations account for the predicament of ethnic groups within nation-states. The authors point out, "The total sociocultural system at any moment in time determines whether the minority will be crushed and exploited, left alone to pursue its own course, or helped in its attempt to advance upwards through the social hierarchy" (1958:273). Wagley and Harris contextualized subject people within a larger web of international relations and external conditions in a clearly anthropological vein nearly half a century before such labels as "world-systems theory," "political economy," and "practice theory" became popular.

In contrast to constructivist theorists, Wagley and Harris were explicitly concerned with the full participation of minority groups in complex societies and their adaptive capacity to achieve new social and ecological niches. To be sure, these authors attribute the position, rank, or status of subordinate collectivities within host societies chiefly to their "cultural preparedness" relative to dominant systems of prestige, national ideals, standards, and norms. They speak of "disabilities" with regard to a minority group's status vis-à-vis the national standards of success, albeit clearly in contextually relative terms (Wagley and Harris 1958:4–6). Furthermore, their perspective is limited by a passive stance and a cultural silence on the part of the members who comprise the subordinate collectivity. Their theory is based on two assumptions. First, subordinated groups seek unconditional socioeconomic and cultural mobility as well as integration into the national hierarchy. Second, acculturation and socioeconomic advancement are controlled entirely by forces that are external to the work of members of the group in question.

This model attributes the plight of minorities to such past and present forces as historical origins, varied physical diacritics and cultural markers, national policies and interests, and global economic and political processes of change that operate above and around members of the group. Wagley and Harris provide a comparative perspective on the genesis, formation, and adaptation of oppressed minority groups. Their approach does not address the circumstances of some ethnic groups who are economically and politically privileged. Furthermore, their paradigm omits the role of both elite and popular agency in building community; they do not, in other words, consider that persons may be actively involved in and conscious of their group's transformation and integration (Kottak and Kozaitis 1999). These limitations notwithstanding, the work of Wagley and Harris provides the foundation for a system of analysis from which contemporary ethnographic accounts of specific ethnic groups might benefit and to which they might contribute.

The anthropological study of ethnic groups has flourished as a legitimate area of research for the past three decades as ethnologists struggle to recapture their place in social research and as they confront worldwide "deterritorialization" of conventional laboratories for ethnographic research (Appadurai 1991; R. Cohen 1978). Global economic shifts and geopolitical transformations during these decades brought about two trends in anthropological research: an increase in the fluidity of traditional contexts and units of ethnographic focus; and intensified attention to local culture as embedded in and affected by its relationship to the state and the world system. Researchers recognized the emergence of indistinct territories and the implications of this change for the traditional localities for ethnographic research that were no longer autonomous, uniform, and static units in time and space (Rouse 1991). Among these changes were the omnipresence of ethnic groups within urban centers and a corresponding shift of anthropological interest in the study of ethnicity as social organization, which involves an analysis of how persons manipulate, manage, and direct cultural features to maintain organizational boundaries vis-à-vis other groups (Barth 1969:9–38; Kozaitis 1993; Nagel 1994).

By the mid-1970s, ethnicity had become a "ubiquitous phenomenon" of which anthropologists were taking notice, in part as a result of decolonization, geopolitical transformations, and participation by ethnic groups in the Civil Rights movement (A. Cohen 1974). As R. Cohen pointed out, ethnicity must be viewed as a critical and timely "problem and focus" in anthropology. To that end, he proposed new theoretical and empirical directions for the discipline (1978:380). A great many anthropological studies appeared, representing some of these new directions, including the sociocultural constitution and subordination of descent-based groups in complex social systems; symbiotic and competitive relations with respect to resources and power among ethnic minorities in nation-states; the role of political elites in the construction of ethnic categories as a source of power and access; and situational expression and construction of ethnic identity and status by ordinary people in a variety of social contexts. These perspectives are not mutually exclusive. Different theories emphasize particular aspects of ethnicity, but they overlap on many substantive points. This discussion therefore serves mainly as an attempt to address the contributions of some of the most influential approaches.

Anthropological studies of ethnic groups usually focus on the characteristics by which such groups may be defined. Ethnologists have tended to emphasize the presumably primordial conditions that define groups. Wagley and Harris (1958:4–10) define ethnic groups in terms of their distinguishing physical and cultural traits that are both different from those of the dominant society and judged by the latter to be inferior. Moreover, the groups are said to be self-conscious social units whose members tend to identify strongly with one another. The groups are usually classified according to rule of descent and are typically endogamous.

Barth (1969) also discusses ethnicity as cultural identity rooted in descent and place. He demonstrates, however, that ethnicity constitutes a form of social organization, the boundaries of which are created, manipulated, and maintained by members of the group to ensure biosocial reproduction. His approach emphasizes the role that humans play

in manipulating cultural content so as to ensure the continuity of ethnic status and identity, in contrast to a strictly biosocial perspective that
defines ethnicity as basically a manifestation of genetics and geography (van den Berghe 1981).

Keyes (1976:204) emphasizes culture as the key feature of ethnicity.
He defines culture as the way people interpret, evaluate, and express
their differences, which he attributes to the "facts of birth." Given such
bases for distinguishing one group from another, Keyes proposes that
genetic makeup, place of birth, and descent (as "abstracted from the
web of kinship") are factors that are "both necessary for and prior to
the existence of ethnic groups" (205). Although he views descent as
the "primordial quality" for membership in an ethnic group, he insists
that cultural traits are associated with genealogical links in ways that
ultimately account for the degree of such membership. As such, an ethnic group is "a type of descent group whose members validate their
claim to shared descent by pointing to cultural attributes which they
believe they hold in common" (208; see also Kozaitis 1987).

Ethnicity may also be viewed as symbolic displays and behavioral
expressions by persons of a given ethnic affiliation "in the pursuit of
their interests vis-à-vis other people who are seen as holding contrasting ethnic identities" (Keyes 1981:10). For example, Keyes contex-
tualizes intergroup relations within the "total political-economy of societies" (11). In addition to the cultural dimension of ethnicity, which
itself is based on blood relations, Keyes emphasizes "the functions of
ethnicity in pursuit of social interests" (14). Ethnicity, then, consists of
"cultural formulations of descent from which people derive their ethnic identities" as well as economically motivated behavior that protects
and reinforces such an identity (14).

The instrumentalist view of ethnic status ascribes such status to those
collectivities that express some patterns of normative behavior, constitute a segment of a larger population, and interact strategically with
people from other sociocultural groups within a larger social system
(Despres 1975). A. Cohen (1974:xi) argues that what people do and "the
degree of conformity by members of the collectivity to those shared
norms in the course of social interaction" are both measures of ethnicity.
Like other theorists of the "resource-competition model" (e.g., Thompson 1989), A. Cohen contends that ethnic collectivities are politically
and economically organized interest groups whose members interact in
a foreign nation-state and compete for strategic resources.

These insights are reinforced by the depiction of ethnicity as "a series of nesting dichotomizations of inclusiveness and exclusiveness." Persons are ethnic by subjective (self-defined) and objective (defined by others) criteria, the process of which depends on particular diacritics that are associated with such membership (R. Cohen 1978:387). Such distinctions are neither necessarily nor exclusively symptomatic of exploitative economic relations between dominant and subordinate groups within the same political context (Vincent 1974). R. Cohen attributes ethnic status to those culturally and physically distinct groups that simply coexist and interact in the same geographical area. He views such groups as neither the products nor the producers of asymmetric relations of power within the same political structure. Rather, diacritics serve as the basis for the construction of boundaries that result in we/they dichotomies.

According to R. Cohen (1978:387), ethnicity consists of "a set of descent-based cultural identities" that are "passed down the generations." A profile of traits and patterns of behavior is subsequently formed and elaborated as persons place themselves, or are placed by others, on the scale of inclusiveness and exclusiveness of real or imagined boundaries. In contrast to the resource-competition model that stresses conflict due to political and economic inequities, R. Cohen (1978:401) proposes that cultural variation may in fact serve as a positive and protective mechanism against contemporary currents of alienation, disconnectedness, and despair. In like manner, Horowitz (1985) argues that self-conscious promotion and expression of cultural traits, rituals, symbols, and beliefs reinforce pride in one's ethnic group and help minimize the alienating effects of marginalization. Ethnic affiliation and sociocultural affinities may be utilized to demand access to strategic resources, political capital, and prestige. Roots, both biological and geographical, combine with cultural orientations to foster the production of identity vis-à-vis other groups, a sense of belonging, and political mobilization among historically subordinated collectivities.

Of equal theoretical significance is the role of political interests and ideological precepts of powerful systems that produce, maintain, and justify the subordination of socioculturally variant groups in complex nation-states (Brass 1985; Smith 1986; B. Williams 1989). Following Wirth's (1961) general concern with cultural hierarchies and differential distribution of power within a single political unit, contemporary authors question the barriers that national ideologies impose on collectivities within the nation and the implications of these barriers for further disenfranchisement. For example, B. Williams (1989:405–6) urges anthropologists to consider "the state as the purveyor of the policies and constraints that both formally and informally direct politically and morally acceptable forms of competition and cooperation." B. Williams believes that "Ethnicity labels the politics of cultural struggle in the nexus of territorial and cultural nationalism that characterizes all putatively homogeneous nation-states. As a label it may sound better than tribe, race, or barbarian, but with respect to political consequences, it still identifies those who are at the borders of the empire" (439).

Ethnicity is resolutely both externally and internally constituted. Ethnic elites, compelled to counteract their core elite counterparts, play a key role in producing myths and creating profiles about "our people." Such strategies ensure their own access to political and economic resources and valorize the cultural customs, rituals, symbols, and beliefs of subordinated ethnic groups (Brass 1985). As I argue elsewhere (Kozaitis 1993, 1997), constructivist approaches to ethnicity emphasize the conclusion that collective resistance to and compliance with host institutions reinforce in ethnic groups an adaptive apparatus that protects and maintains their organizational solidarity, identity, and meaning. Situational manipulation of ethnic boundaries facilitates the construction of desirable identity, strengthens intragroup relations, and fosters resourceful negotiations with respect to economic, political, and social mobility (Barth 1969; Nagel 1994; Okamura 1981). The decolonization of the Third World gave rise to nationalistic and ethnic consciousness. The end of communism in Europe, however, has ushered in a transnational consciousness whereby constructed, flexible, and mobilized ethnicity finds a home in multiple localities, layers of expression, and degrees of scale in the world system.

THE ETHNIC GROUP AS A UNIT
OF ANTHROPOLOGICAL ANALYSIS AND PRAXIS

Four decades of anthropological studies on the nature and culture of ethnic groups have led to the conclusion that ethnicity is best understood within the parameters of larger historical events, global political and economic transformations, state policies, local action within and between social groups, and local systems of meaning that both prohibit and foster group status and survival. The theory of ethnicity proposed here as conscious adaptation is integrative and holistic in its approach to the study of ethnic groups (Kozaitis 1993, 1997). It builds on assumptions of ecological anthropology by borrowing and synthesizing ideas and methods of analysis from political economy and practice theory. This approach begins and ends with an ethnographic description of daily life as members of a collective express it behaviorally, symbolically, and ideationally within the parameters of a physical environment and a social context. It recognizes, however, that this local view of life is also embedded in a web of intra- and extra-group historical, political, and economic relations and is subject to ongoing change.

This framework is, like practice theory, fundamentally concerned with internal dynamics of local culture and with people as active producers of culture. Conscious adaptation, however, differs from practice theory, which insists on an absolute interdependency of internal and external forces. It affiliates instead with political economy for its emphasis on causality, process, and outcome. This analysis of local change therefore remains epistemologically deterministic. It assumes that the social organization of a given ethnic group is necessarily shaped and directed by historical incidents, by society, by ecological constraints and opportunities, and by political inequality that dominant external systems impose on internal order.

Conscious adaptation contributes several principles to sociocultural theory in general and to ethnicity theory in particular. First, it fosters regard for the level of sociocultural complexity that contemporary ethnic groups and transnational communities embody (i.e., cultural hybridism, rather than cultural authenticity, characterizes these social categories). Second, it allows us to deal with cumulative experience as it affects sociocultural adaptation, insofar as members of endemic ethnic groups have learned from long-term interactions with dominant social systems what does and does not work to ensure biological and sociocultural continuity in both particular environments and in a variety of diaspora contexts. Third, it leads us to an appreciation for the level of cognitive sophistication relative to world view and world status that contemporary ethnic groups possess, since contemporary informants demonstrate high competence and performance in the acquisition, interpretation, and application of knowledge relative to their collective past, present, and future.

Anthropologists must decide on the particular angle from which we may contribute scientifically and responsibly to the study of ethnicity and of the adaptation, reproduction, and security of ethnic groups. We must remember that, as is true of all rigorous social and cultural inquiry, the study of ethnic groups is intrinsically political and consequential in its conception, design, and focus. As Wagley and Harris (1958:294) asserted more than forty years ago, "The fundamental motivation of anyone interested in reading about, writing about, or studying minority groups is ultimately the practical application of this knowledge to alleviate the plight of those who suffer disadvantages of one kind or another as members of minority groups."

The anthropology-as-praxis approach treats research, theory, and action as key features of a single project. This approach requires organic intellectual work, not simply academic efficiency. It relies on collaboration among anthropologists and other scientists, not competition between politically charged theoretical factions. It insists on authentic, lateral partnerships with research participants, not hierarchical patron-client relations. And finally, and perhaps most critically, anthropology proper is grounded today in public engagement, not in private interests. This paradigm is especially plausible in the anthropology of ethnic groups, many of which many are forced to live precariously in a world system that threatens and neglects local community life and health. Ethnicity is a global phenomenon, a local experience, and a personal struggle. Ethnic groups the world over seek human worth, economic security, and political legitimacy. In the tradition of all social and cultural collectivities, ethnic groups have done, and continue to do, their part in ensuring these rights and privileges for anthropologists. The least we can do is to reciprocate in kind.

REFERENCES

Appadurai, A. 1991. Global Ethnoscapes: Notes and Queries for a Transnational Anthropology. In *Recapturing Anthropology: Working in the Present*, ed. R. Fox, 191–210. Santa Fe, N.M.: School of American Research.

Barth, F. 1969. Introduction. In *Ethnic Groups and Boundaries: The Social Organization of Cultural Difference*, ed. F. Barth, 9–38. Boston: Little, Brown.

Bourdieu, P. 1977. *Outline of a Theory of Practice*, trans. R. Nice. Cambridge: Cambridge University Press.

Brass, P., ed. 1985. *Ethnic Groups and the State*. London: Croom Helm.

Cohen, A. 1974. The Lesson of Ethnicity. In *Urban Ethnicity*, ed. A. Cohen, ix–xxiii. London: Tavistock.

Cohen, R. 1978. Ethnicity: Problem and Focus in Anthropology. *Annual Review of Anthropology* 7:379–403.

Despres, L. 1975. Toward a Theory of Ethnic Phenomena. In *Ethnicity and Resource Competition in Plural Societies*, ed. L. Despres, 100–122. The Hague: Mouton.

Glazer, N., and D. Moynihan. 1976. *Ethnicity: Theory and Experience*. Cambridge: Harvard University Press.

Horowitz, D. 1985. *Ethnic Groups in Conflict*. Berkeley: University of California Press.

Keyes, C. 1976. Towards a New Formulation of the Concept of Ethnic Group. *Ethnicity* 3(3):202–13.

———. 1981. The Dialectic of Ethnic Change. In *Ethnic Change*, ed. C. Keyes, pp. 3–30. Seattle: University of Washington Press.

Kottak, C., and K. Kozaitis. 1999. *On Being Different: Diversity and Multiculturalism in the North American Mainstream*. New York: McGraw Hill.

Kozaitis, K. 1987. Being Old and Greek in America. In *Ethnic Dimensions of Aging*, ed. D. Gelfand and C. Barresi, 179–95. New York: Springer.

———. 1993. Conscious Adaptation: Change in Perpetuity among the Roma of Athens, Greece. Ph.D. dissertation, University of Michigan.

———. 1997. Foreigners among Foreigners: Social Organization among the Roma of Athens, Greece. *Urban Anthropology* 26(2):165–99.

Nagel, J. 1994. Constructing Ethnicity: Creating and Recreating Ethnic Identity and Culture. *Social Problems* 41(1):152–76.

Okamura, J. 1981. Situational Ethnicity. *Ethnic and Racial Studies* 4(4):452–65.

Ortner, S. 1984. Anthropological Theory since the Sixties. *Comparative Studies in Society and History* 26(1):126–66.

Roseberry, W. 1988. Political Economy. *Annual Review of Anthropology* 17:161–85.

———. 1989. *Anthropologies and Histories: Essays in Culture, History, and Political Economy*. New Brunswick, N.J.: Rutgers University Press.

Rouse, R. 1991. Mexican Migration and the Social Space of Postmodernism. *Diaspora* 1(1):8–23.

Smith, A., ed. 1986. *The Ethnic Origin of Nations*. Oxford: Basil Blackwell.

Thompson, R. 1989. *Theories of Ethnicity*. New York: Greenwood.

Van den Berghe, P. 1981. *The Ethnic Phenomenon*. New York: Elsevier.

Vincent, J. 1974. The Structuring of Ethnicity. *Human Organization* 33(4):375–90.

Wagley, C., and M. Harris. 1958. *Minorities in the New World: Six Case Studies*. New York: Columbia University Press.

Wallerstein, E. 1979. *The Capitalist World Economy*. New York: Cambridge University Press.

Williams, B. 1989. A Class Act: Anthropology and the Race to Nation across Ethnic Terrain. *Annual Review of Anthropology* 18:401–44.

Williams, R. 1982. *The Sociology of Culture*. New York: Schocken.

Wirth, L. 1961. *The Politics of Cultural Pluralism*. Madison: University of Wisconsin Press.

Wolf, E. 1982. *Europe and the People without History*. Berkeley: University of California Press.

Comparative Perspectives on International Migration: Illegals or "Guest Workers" in the American South?

Eric C. Jones and Robert E. Rhoades

The subject of international migration stands at the nexus of many forces—political, economic, cultural, institutional—that define relations among nation-states. The individual and societal costs and benefits of international labor migration have been the subject of a large body of social science research (Castles and Kosack 1985; Castles and Miller 1998; Rhoades 1996). Individuals and their families may benefit from migration, but the regions that send migrants collectively lose their youngest, most able-bodied, and most skilled workers. They also become dependent on economies far away (Amin 1974; Rhoades 1978b). Businesses and employers in receiving societies may benefit from cutting labor costs in the short run, but the receiving economy often builds up its own economic dependence on the migrant population's purchasing power. During periods of economic recession, ethnic and labor tensions frequently arise between native workers and migrants (Carmon 1996; Portes 1978; Wiest 1979). The trade-offs are significant and hotly debated by the many stakeholder groups impacted by the process. With globalization and increasing lowering of trade barriers, it is expected that international labor migration (including both legal and illegal movements) will continue at even higher rates in the decades to come (Castles and Miller 1998; Kearney 1995). Viable and just policies are desperately needed for countries that import labor as well as for those that export workers.

This essay examines two examples of international labor migration: Germany's *Gastarbeiter* ("guest workers") and recent "illegal" migrants from Latin America to the U.S. South. The comparison is of interest due to the continuing debate in the United States over immigration policy, which is influenced by considerations such as labor needs in certain occupations, border sharing, Hispanic political power in the United States, and various related human rights issues. U.S. immigration policy has at different times included the building of fences along portions of the 2,000-mile border with Mexico, imposing a quota system, stimulating development of border industries, deporting illegals, and levying heavy fines on U.S. firms employing illegal labor. All of these measures have been highly controversial and have been frequently modified. A "guest worker" approach has never been fully implemented, although many constituencies in the United States have called on the government to consider it in light of its purported humanitarian, social, and economic benefits. An anthropologically informed comparison of labor migration to Germany and the United States would therefore be highly useful in the ongoing policy debate. Immigration in these two situations can be compared according to civil or political rights, migration streams, ethnic adaptations and conflict, and return migration and remittances—all issues that have been well documented in the anthropological migration literature (Massey et al. 1994). We present the broad similarities and differences with an eye on policy and the situation of the new Hispanic immigration into the U.S. South. We review Germany's temporary guest-worker programs and the U.S. labor-migrant experiences and then compare the two cases in light of attempts to create a guest-worker program in the U.S. South.

THE ANTHROPOLOGY OF LABOR MIGRATION

The earliest anthropological studies of migration focused on culture clashes at local levels within the "little community" tradition of anthropology (Lewis 1959; Park 1928; Redfield, Linton, and Herskovits 1936). During the 1960s and 1970s, there was a surge in interest in the anthropology of migration with a focus on the migration processes of adaptation, acculturation, integration, and assimilation (Ablon 1964; Abu-Lughod 1961; Butterworth 1974). Most of this work was carried out in a relatively timeless conceptual framework based on short fieldwork periods either in the rural originating areas or in the urban receiving contexts. In addition, much of this literature emphasized the migrants, rather than the historical, structural, and socioeconomic forces governing migration. Migration was therefore linked neither to regional and world economic trends nor to labor cycles, although those matters were ultimately dealt with by studies framed in terms of modernization theory (du Toit and Safa 1975; Todaro 1969) and "core-periphery" dependency theory (Castles and Kosack 1985; Philpott 1973; Rhoades 1978a). The importance of pursuing multi-sited, integrative analysis of immigration at various levels (i.e., local, national, and international) has increased in recent years due to advancing globalization processes (Massey et al. 1994; Portes 1997). Without a transnational and integrative approach, policy may be (mis)informed by erratic public opinion on immigration rather than by systematic scientific data.

Labor migration is typically cyclical and involves a return phase, or multiple phases; it cannot be described as a single event. It must be seen against the larger background of socio-demographic processes and intraregional linkages over a long time frame (Boehning 1974). In all cases of cyclical migration in post-industrial economies, a substantial portion of the migrant population that intended to return to the sending region does not do so for a number of reasons (Waldorf 1995). Like most migrants, they grow accustomed to higher standards of living, higher wages, better education, and better health care opportunities. They may also be unable to save as much money as they had expected. They thus postpone their return and often bring their dependents (mainly wives and children in cases of male labor migration) to them rather than go back to those families (Boehning 1974). Guest-worker programs are designed specifically to encourage the temporary, cyclical, return-oriented style of migration.

Reviews of the literature on return migration (Gmelch 1980; King 1979, 1986) and on migration and development (Kearney 1986; Safa and du Toit 1975) indicate that return migrants typically convert their earnings into consumption items, especially housing and education, and do not invest in rural production in the sending areas largely because of the lack of investment opportunity. Remittances to families left back home, mainly the elderly and very young, are utilized for subsistence and often result in removing people from rural productive enterprises. Nonetheless, arguments have been made that dependency theory does not seem to explain recent Mexico-U.S. migration, since it generates considerable economic activity in Mexican communities under certain conditions (Durand et al. 1996). The return phenomenon is fairly well documented in the case of intra-European migration, and studies of return to Mexico from the United States indicate patterns similar to those of Europe (Massey and Espinosa 1997).

Germany: Policies of a "Non-Immigrant Nation"

The guest-worker program in Germany has been in effect since 1955. (See, however, Rhoades 1978a for a historical analysis of Germany's use of foreign labor since the late nineteenth century.) It was a carefully designed state policy meant to recruit and rotate workers on a temporary, as-needed basis through a narrowly defined industrial labor market. Over the years, however, the experience proved to be neither temporary nor free of social costs. Social analysts now refer to a "foreign worker problem," which involves illegal migration, human rights abuses, ethnic conflict, and other social ills. The program was designed to provide cheap labor and to avoid the permanent social integration of foreign workers, who were not originally intended to receive social services support. During periods of economic recession, the employers and the German government had the power to return workers to their homelands, thus exporting their unemployment problem. Following the recession of 1972–73, Germany stopped formal recruitment of workers and did not reintroduce the program until 1989—although by that date a rather large resident population, including families of the workers, had settled permanently in the country. Illegal immigration was rampant, and refugees (including ethnic Germans from eastern Europe) continued to enter the country.

The native German population has experienced negative growth in recent decades, due to low birth rates. As a result, aging foreign nationals make up a higher percentage of the German work force and labor union membership as compared with other post-industrial nations (Edye 1987; Fassman and Munz 1992). Foreign labor recruitment was halted in 1973, and immigration controls were increased, but the number of foreigners in Germany continued to grow due to the reunification of workers' families and to births of foreign workers' children. The Federal Republic of Germany saw its foreign resident population grow from 1.1 percent in 1950 to 8.2 percent in 1990 (Fassman and Munz 1992). Unified Germany now has a permanent immigrant population, accounting for over 75 percent of all migrant Turks, Greeks, eastern and central Europeans, and Yugoslavians, plus about 33 percent of all migrant Italians and Spaniards currently in European Community nations (Fassman and Munz 1992). Foreigners now make up around 8 percent of unified Germany (Martin 1994), although they constitute approximately 10 percent of the work force.

Compared with the general German population, foreigners are younger, tend to have larger families, live in blighted urban areas, and have a more outdoor socializing style. These factors have led to tensions between "guests" and German nationals, as well as a great deal of prejudice based on stereotypes. It was expected that after the reunification of the nation, Germany's industrial core would receive more politically and ethnically acceptable labor from the former East Germany and would thus have to rely less on southern European, Slavic, and Turkish labor. There still remains, however, a structural labor shortage in many menial occupations, requiring continued recruitment of foreigners.

Germany's latest iteration of a guest-worker program involves seasonal labor, work-and-learn apprenticeships, firm-to-firm subcontracting, and frontier worker initiatives. Laborers recruited through these routes, however, still make up only one-seventh of Germany's foreign workers (Martin 1994). Racial and ethnic tensions run high between foreigners and working-class Germans, especially in the relatively economically depressed former East Germany, and violence has erupted on a number of notable occasions. The bottom line is that Germany's guest-worker programs, which were supposed to be temporary, have become permanent features of the economy, resulting in a multicultural society, with all the problems attendant on such heterogeneity.

The United States: Braceros *and the* Undocumented *"Problem" in an Immigrant Nation*

The so-called problem of Mexican migration into the United States is as old as the southern border itself. The international political boundary is crisscrossed and blurred through historical, cultural, and kinship ties, a fact that makes the border unsuccessful in keeping citizens legally on either side. In reality, both countries have virtually pursued the equivalent of an open-door policy in response to the demand for cheap labor. From its inception in the nineteenth century until the present, "restrictive immigration legislation . . . never represented, in their proposals or practice, an effective deterrent to the continued flow of undocumented workers from Mexico to the United States" (Bustamante 1978:332). The lack of documentation has resulted in census counts that amount to only half the probable Hispanic population levels in Georgia (Rodriguez 1999), and probably in most of the South as well.

The migrant flows now originate in rural areas in Central and South America as well as Mexico, so that the problem of undocumented labor in the United States is more complex than just a U.S.-Mexico issue. Like migrants to Germany from eastern and southern Europe, the Mexican and other Latin American migrants have kept an eye on the border as a gateway to higher wages earned through mainly seasonal employment, both legal and illegal. Millions of legal migrants have come to the United States through a variety of programs. The first *bracero*, or laborer, program in the United States, lasting from 1917 to 1922, was aimed at recruiting temporary workers, who were expected to return home. Only about half of them, however, actually returned to Mexico. Between 1942 and 1962, a bilateral agreement between the United States and Mexico constituted a second *bracero* program, while Mexican border states simultaneously became permanent home bases for migrants.

To this day, northern Mexico continues to be a stepping stone for southern Mexican migrants, while northern Mexicans are increasingly tied to NAFTA-inspired *maquiladoras*, or assembly plants. While *bracero* programs have attracted millions of workers to the United States, illegal migration has been a more substantial source of labor. It is estimated that illegal migrants now account for approximately 10 percent of foreign-born laborers in the United States, twice the level of 1970, although less than the estimated 14 percent reported at the beginning of the century (Schuck 1998). Whether the migration is legal or illegal, it has flowed from labor-redundant areas in Mexico to labor-demanding areas in the United States at a constant rate for well over 150 years. Georgia's Hispanic population remains a low 2.9 percent of the total population of the state, although it has been estimated to be actually as high as 6.3 percent (Rodriguez 1999); nevertheless, it is growing at a much faster rate than the average increase for the country as a whole.

The only U.S. program that resembles the German guest-worker approach is that for migrants holding H-2 visa status. The number of work-ers in this class is small, but an examination of their situation is illumi-nating; see, for example Griffith's (1986) study of legal Jamaican tem-porary workers. The terms of the H-2 program specify that a company is legally required first to advertise around the United States before re-cruiting outsiders. The company must then engage in an expensive and difficult application program, which includes guaranteeing that trans-portation and housing costs will be covered. In many ways, these re-quirements are similar to those that governed the recruitment of for-eign workers to Germany throughout the 1960s and 1970s. In the United States, xenophobia has been giving way to guest-worker-type propos-als; the agricultural industry in California has been particularly vocal in championing such programs. The South is also heavily reliant on mi-grant labor for seasonal agricultural work, as well as for industrial hog and chicken farms and plants (Griffith 1993; Stull, Broadway, and Griffith 1995). Migration to the South offers an excellent laboratory for comparison between the United States and Germany, given the very recent influx of Hispanics into an area that had few labor migrants as late as the 1980s.

COMPARATIVE OBSERVATIONS:
GERMANY AND THE UNITED STATES

The emergence of a migrant presence in the South is strikingly similar to the process that brought migrants to Germany in the 1950s. The liv-ing conditions of the migrants in both situations are comparable. Turk-ish and Spanish migrants moved into low-value, run-down inner-city housing or factory barracks in Germany, while Hispanics in Georgia typically have been housed in dilapidated mobile home parks or "single-wide" mobile homes provided by employers. At first, single males come alone in a form of chain migration, and they are often managed on the work site by an overseer who speaks their language. After a while, the men bring their families and set up more stable living arrangements. Migrant businesses emerge to cater to their interests (especially restau-rants, grocery stores, hardware stores, taxis, and bus lines). The num-ber of Hispanic businesses has grown rapidly in Georgia in the past ten years; it is now estimated at more than 13,000 (Paulette and Leftwich 1999).

The migrant enclaves, whether in Stuttgart, Germany, or Gainesville,

Georgia, are similar in their capacity to fulfill functional migrant needs. Newspapers appear in the language of the migrants, and voluntary social and sports clubs come into being. When the migrant population becomes visible (around 12 percent of the local population), however, tensions tend to arise. These tensions can lead to such actions as the local government's attempting to ban use of any but the native language.

Despite these general similarities, there are numerous differences between the two situations, an analysis of which might help clarify immigration policy, labor demand, migrant streams, and ethnic relations.

Policies, Rights, and Citizenship

Citizenship, amnesty, and refugee policies are tools by which the state manages the flows of labor resources while constrained by ethnic relations, international relations, and economic conditions. As such, economic entitlements (e.g., being allowed to work and pay taxes) are granted long before social rights (e.g., right to welfare benefits), let alone political rights (e.g., right to vote) (Guiraudon 1998). The manner in which full citizenship is granted is the main difference between the United States and Germany. The basis of U.S. citizenship is birth on U.S. soil or birth to someone who is already a citizen. In Germany, the basis of citizenship is birth to a descendant of a registered German, whether or not that person lives in Germany. Moreover, the United States relies heavily on amnesty, whereas Germany has relied more on foreign labor policies. The status of family, naturalization, and asylum is similar. The U.S. Congress has recently been looking at reducing visa priority for adult siblings and children while increasing priorities for minors and parents. Access to most social and economic benefits seems to be similar in both countries, except in the matter of the opportunity to receive credit and in the risk of union organizing.

Labor Demand and Worker Competition and Cooperation

Pressures on workers will affect unionization, ethnic conflict, and occupation. Factories and construction companies were occupational destinations for migrants to Germany. The strength of unions may be a causal factor in the difference in rights enjoyed by immigrants in the two countries. In the southern United States, construction and landscaping businesses are large employers of semi-skilled labor. Unskilled labor opportunities include picking oranges in Florida, harvesting cucumbers in North Carolina, working in carpet mills in Georgia, and toiling in poultry plants in Georgia, Alabama, and Arkansas. Southern industry is also booming due to post-NAFTA export increases to Mexico.

Migration Flows and Streams

Source and destination characteristics are partially determined by the maturity, size, and regularity of migration flows, as well as by flows from other regions and countries. The basis for the difference between agents of recruitment in the United States and Germany seems to be that the United States holds employers legally responsible for assessing the availability of worker housing and transportation.[1] Employers thus seek out and recruit illegal workers who are willing to do without the legal niceties. On the other hand, German companies are mandated to pay recruitment fees by the government. To maintain this flow of funds, the politicians are forced to play a role in migrant recruitment efforts.

Ethnicity

We suggest that in-group formation will be affected by migration-stream characteristics, perceived differences between groups, and general economic pressures. In Germany, urban Turks show little fellowship with rural Turks (Mandel 1994). In the United States, illegal immigrants are motivated to assimilate, and many thus develop discriminatory feelings toward potential immigrants, including those from their own ethnic group or nationality. This feeling usually remains impersonal and abstract and does not carry over into personal networks; people are willing to help new immigrants, especially those who are considered family. Upon return to the home country, Mexican migrants typically receive respect due to their new wealth; this factor is much less pronounced among those who return from working in Germany.

CONCLUSION

Over the years, the United States has relied haphazardly on amnesty rather than directed labor immigration policies. In May of 1998, Hispanics working their way from Florida to New York were granted temporary amnesty by the U.S. Immigration and Naturalization Service in order to harvest Georgia's Vidalia onions; they were then expected to return home. Colorado ski areas have pushed for the same preferential use of amnesty rights. Will this system continue to serve U.S. labor needs and domestic politics, or is the German experience a model for the U.S. South?

Using cases of Spanish or Turkish migrants returning from Germany and Mexicans returning from the United States, future research could ascertain the circumstances under which return migration affords a better quality of life to migrants and under what circumstances migration or return migration bolsters the economies of the sending countries (Durand et al. 1996). Moreover, the predictability of return migration and its impact on the home communities should be explored in terms of formal political structures. For example, a theory explaining the known relationship between recession and return migration might include the idea that actual behavior is largely predicted by individual demographic variables and job satisfaction in the short term (Waldorf 1995), whereas long-term trajectories involve intergroup and international relations, structural changes in a world capitalist system, and the cumulative effects of stepwise, return, and aging migration streams.

Because immigrants have taken up the lower echelon of jobs, industrial and post-industrial societies have become accustomed to international migration. Nonetheless, the lack of government backlash or crackdown on immigration (Joppke 1998) looks peculiar to the casual onlooker, in light of observable nationalistic sentiments. Why have governments not responded more harshly? Do classical notions of native-immigrant job competition and ethnic conflict (e.g., Ku Klux Klan action in Dalton, Georgia, in 1998) not bring anything to bear on our understanding of the phenomenon of migration? Freeman (1998) analyzed policy outcomes and found little basis for the trendy arguments that the state is withering away or losing control over sovereignty and citizenship as a result of international migration.

Despite policy differences between Germany and the United States, it is possible that a German-like guest-worker program would be effective in the United States to the extent that it might stem illegal immigration. Further comparative analysis has the potential to highlight the structural similarities and differences critical to any adaptation of a guest-worker model in this country. It is already instructive to note that

Germany does not consider itself a country of immigrants. The U.S. "melting pot," on the other hand, has had little coherence in foreign labor policy. The repercussions of these tendencies for race relations, discrimination, and ethnic conflict as a result of the implementation of policies similar to Germany's would be another, possibly bleaker, story.

NOTES

Particular thanks to Mika Cohen for her review of this manuscript. The authors are solely responsible for any oversights and omissions

1. In the early guest-worker period (1950s, early 1960s), many German companies also housed workers in factory housing.

REFERENCES

Ablon, J. 1964. Relocated American Indians in the San Francisco Bay Area. *Human Organization* 23:296–304.

Abu-Lughod, L. 1961. Migrant Adjustment to City Life: The Egyptian Case. *American Journal of Sociology* 47:22–32.

Amin, J. 1974. *Neo-Colonialism in West Africa*, trans. F. McDonagh. New York: Monthly Review Press.

Boehning, W. 1974. The Economic Effects of the Employment of Foreign Workers, with Special Reference to the Labor Markets of Europe's Post-Industrial Countries. In *The Effects of the Employment of Foreign Workers*, ed. W. Boehning and D. Maillat, 41–123. Paris: OECD.

Bustamante, J. 1978. The Mexicans Are Coming. *International Migration Review* 17(2):323–41.

Butterworth, D. 1974. Two Small Groups: A Comparison of Migrants and Non-Migrants in Mexico City. *Urban Anthropology* 1:29–50.

Carmon, N. 1996. *Post-Industrial Societies: Theoretical Analysis and Policy-Related Research*. New York: St. Martin's Press.

Castles, S., and G. Kosack. 1985. *Immigrant Workers and Class Structure in Western Europe*. 2d ed. Oxford: Oxford University Press.

Castles, S., and M. Miller. 1998. *The Age of Migration: International Population Movements in the Modern World*. 2d ed. New York: Guilford.

Durand, J., W. Kandel, E. Parrado, and D. Massey. 1996. International Migration and Development in Mexican Communities. *Demography* 33(2):249–64.

Du Toit, B., and H. Safa, eds. 1975. *Migration and Urbanization: Models and Adaptive Strategies*. The Hague: Mouton.

Edye, D. 1987. *Immigrant Labor and Government Policy: The Cases of the Federal Republic of Germany and France.* Brookfield, Vt.: Gower.

Fassman, H., and R. Munz. 1992. Patterns and Trends of International Migration in Western Europe. *Population and Development Review* 18:457–80.

Freeman, G. 1998. The Decline of Sovereignty? Politics and Immigration Restriction in Liberal States. In *Challenge to the Nation-State: Immigration in Western Europe and the United States*, ed. C. Joppke, 25–50. New York: Oxford University Press.

Gmelch, G. 1980. Return Migration. *Annual Review of Anthropology* 9:135–59.

Griffith, D. 1986. Peasants in Reserve: Temporary West Indian Labor in the U.S. Labor Market. *International Migration Review* 20(4):875–98.

———. 1993. *Jones' Minimal: Low-Wage Labor in the United States.* Albany: State University of New York Press.

Guiraudon, V. 1998. Citizenship Rights for Non-Citizens: France, Germany, and the Netherlands. In *Challenge to the Nation-State: Immigration in Western Europe and the United States*, ed. C. Joppke, 51–62. New York: Oxford University Press.

Joppke, C., ed. 1998. *Challenge to the Nation-State: Immigration in Western Europe and the United States.* New York: Oxford University Press.

Kearney, M. 1986. From the Invisible Hand to Visible Feet: Anthropological Studies of Migration and Development. *Annual Review of Anthropology* 15:331–61.

———. 1995. The Local and the Global: The Anthropology of Globalization and Transnationalism. *Annual Review of Anthropology* 24:547–65.

King, R. 1979. Return Migration: A Review of Some Case Studies from Southern Europe. *Mediterranean Studies* 1:30–35.

———. 1986. Return Migration and Regional Economic Development: An Overview. In *Return Migration and Return Economic Problems*, ed. R. King, 1–37. Dover, N.H.: Croom Helm.

Lewis, O. 1959. *Five Families: Mexican Case Studies in the Culture of Poverty.* New York: Basic Books.

Mandel, R. 1994. Fortress Europe and the Foreigners Within: Germany's Turks. In *The Anthropology of Europe: Identities and Boundaries in Conflict*, ed. V. Goddard, J. Lobera, and C. Shore, 113–24. Providence, R.I.: Berg.

Martin, P. 1994. *Migration and Trade: Challenges for the 1990s.* Berkeley: University of California Press.

Massey, D., J. Arango, G. Hugo, A. Kouaouci, A. Pellegrino, and J. Taylor. 1994. An Evaluation of International Migration Theory: The North American Case. *Population and Development Review* 20(4):699–751.

Massey, D., and K. Espinosa. 1997. What's Driving Mexico–U.S. Migration:

A Theoretical, Empirical, and Policy Analysis. *American Journal of Sociology* 102(4):939–99.

Park, R. 1928. Human Migration and the Marginal Man. *American Journal of Sociology* 33(6):881–93.

Paulette, G., and G. Leftwich. 1999. Georgia's Piñata. *Georgia Trend*, November, 24.

Philpott, S. 1973. *West Indian Migration: The Montserrat Case*. London: Athlone.

Portes, A. 1978. Migration and Underdevelopment. *Politics and Society* 8:1–48.

———. 1997. Immigration Theory for a New Century: Some Problems and Opportunities. *International Migration Review* 31:799–825.

Redfield, R., R. Linton, and M. Herskovits. 1936. Memorandum for the Study of Acculturation. *American Anthropologist* 38:149–52.

Rhoades, R. 1978a. Foreign Labor and German Industrial Capitalism, 1871–1978: The Evolution of a Migratory System. *American Ethnologist* 5(3): 553–73.

———. 1978b. Intra-European Return Migration and Rural Development: Lessons from the Spanish Case. *Human Organization* 37:137–48.

———. 1996. European Cyclical Migration and Economic Development: The Case of Southern Spain. In *Urban Life: Readings in Urban Anthropology*, 3d ed., ed. G. Gmelch and W. Zenner, 30–48. Prospect Heights, Ill.: Waveland.

Rodriguez, Y. GSU Says Hispanic Numbers Way Off. *Atlanta Constitution*, October 5, A5.

Safa, H., and B. du Toit, eds. 1975. *Migration and Development: Implications for Ethnic Identity and Political Conflict*. The Hague: Mouton.

Schuck, P. 1998. The Legal Rights of Citizens and Aliens in the United States. In *Temporary Workers or Future Citizens?* ed. M. Weiner and T. Hanami, 238–90. New York: New York University Press.

Stull, D., M. Broadway, and D. Griffith. 1995. *Any Way You Cut It: Meat Processing and Small-Town America*. Lawrence: University Press of Kansas.

Todaro, M. 1969. *Internal Migration in Developing Countries: A Review of Theory*. Geneva: International Labor Organization.

Waldorf, B. 1995. Determinants of International Return Migrants' Intentions. *Professional Geographer* 47:125–36.

Wiest, R. 1979. Anthropological Perspectives on Return Migration: A Critical Commentary. *Papers in Anthropology* 20:167–87.

How Many Are There?
Ethnographic Estimates of
Mexican Women in Atlanta, Georgia

Martha W. Rees

Mexican immigrants, both documented and undocumented, are hard to count. Because of their history with U.S. officialdom, many are not counted or are missed in national and local censuses. This essay presents an estimate of the number of Mexican women in Atlanta, Georgia, based on census and official figures, survey data, and ethnographic data. The survey data are based on interviews with male and female Mexican migrants in Atlanta in 1998.[1]

Information available to us about Mexican female migrants is even more limited than that about the population as a whole. In order to understand the characteristics of this new migration, we have to understand the general context of Mexican female migration, in terms of the multiple factors in Mexico, in the United States, and in the world economy in general that contribute to it.

Much of the research on Mexican migration describes male migration and remittances, or those sent back to Mexico; there are few studies of female migrants, with the notable exceptions of those by Hondagneu-Sotelo (1994) and Donato (1992). Most of the literature assumes that male migration is an individual income-maximizing strategy, although Massey et al. (1994) present a cogent criticism of this neoliberal approach. Remittances to Mexico form the third largest source of foreign exchange in that country. The increasing tendency of women to migrate to the United States to join their husbands indicates that for many Mexican migrants, household and family considerations still affect behavior. In order to understand migration, we have to take women's activities into account, both at home and as migrants. Women's work (or potential to work) as migrants may also play a role in female migration and in their activities as migrants. Explanations that do not take women's work into account, and that treat the household as a homogeneous unit or migration as a purely individual behavior, are not adequate. The work of Stephen (1990) and Collins (1988) tell us something about conditions at home for the female head of a migrant household. They show that male migration leads to increased female participation in agriculture and that women's work at home supports male migration (Rees 1998).

More Mexican families and more single women now migrate to the United States (Cornelius 1991:170; see also Woo-Morales 1995). Conditions in Mexico contribute to migration; the Mexican crisis began in the early 1980s and brought about important changes in the state and civil society (Jenkins 1977). In 1986, the price of petroleum fell, and Mexico suffered negative economic growth and three-digit inflation for the first time in three decades (INEGI 1992). One of the effects of the crisis was lowered wages, which fell to their lowest point in 1987. Recovery of international confidence came at the cost of salary increases and social subsidies. Economic conditions worsened, and the potential for social unrest increased. The crisis and restructuring could easily have encouraged both male and female labor to move from sites of low wages in Mexico to higher-wage areas in the United States in the 1980s.

Conditions in the United States likewise influence Mexican immigration. As wages fell in this country and production continued its move to cheaper labor sites, often in Mexico, the U.S. labor market became increasingly service-oriented. Both lower wages and the demand for service labor helped create a demand for low-skilled, cheap labor (Castells 1980). U.S. immigration laws do not stop the flow but rather affect the price and condition of labor (Bustamante, Reynolds, and Hinojosa Ojeda 1992).

Whether a Mexican woman migrant works may also depend on her total household income (number of workers) and composition (number of small children) (Donato 1992). Nevertheless, more Mexican female migrants work. The participation of Hispanic women in the U.S. labor market (which overall includes non-Mexicans and nonmigrants) increased 14 percent between 1960 and 1980 (Stier and Tienda 1992).[2] Once in the United States, their resources, potential income (including spouse's income), and language skills influence whether they work. This work is not just in agriculture, the traditional employment of Mexican migrants. Hispanic women who engage in non-agricultural work have higher levels of education than farm workers and tend to be single. Pedraza-Bailey conducted a survey of Mexican female migrants who entered the United States between 1960 and 1970. At the time of that survey, 34 percent were working in small services, 28 percent were in industries such as textiles, 17 percent were in primary industries such as agriculture, and the remaining 21 percent were skilled workers, professionals, or bureaucrats (Pedraza-Bailey 1985:111-13). In another study more than 65 percent of U.S. migrants from Oaxaca worked in non-agricultural jobs (Luque González and Corona Cuapio 1992).

In conclusion, Mexican migration to the United States can be explained only by examining multiple local, national, and world factors. The same can be said specifically of female migration, albeit with some specific differences that have to do with women's households, activities in Mexico, networks, and other resources, including education. Household migration may increase if there is work for both spouses, which seems to be the case in Atlanta, with its high demand for workers in services, meatpacking, and other activities, including domestic service.

Atlanta is the largest urban center in the southeastern United States. Since the 1980s, the region has undergone profound social, cultural, and demographic change. The region has traditionally been home to two main ethnic groups: African Americans and European Americans. In the 1970s and 1980s, however, over 10,000 migrants and refugees from Vietnam arrived in the Atlanta area, changing the ethnic makeup of the region and affecting a variety of political, economic, and social relations (CARA 1996b).

Mexican migration to the United States took off in the 1980s. From 1980 to 1995, the Hispanic population of Georgia grew 130 percent. By 1996 there were 462,973 Hispanics in Georgia. There are no figures on the number of Hispanics who are Mexican; estimates from centers that deal with Hispanics indicate that about 90 percent of the Hispanics are Mexican. In order to be on the conservative side, I use the figure of 80 percent. The number of Hispanics who are women is even more difficult to ascertain. Many Mexicans are undocumented; women in particular tend to be undocumented, which makes them especially difficult to count.

The Hispanic population of Georgia has grown especially in the metropolitan area of Atlanta, made up of Fulton, De Kalb, Gwinnett, Cobb, and Cherokee Counties; Clayton, Rockdale, Henry, Douglas, and Fayette Counties were added to the metropolitan area in 1996. The number of Hispanics in this region grew from 30,000 in 1982 to over 110,000 in 1992, an increase of 260 percent in ten years. Between 1992 and 1996, the Hispanic population of the Atlanta metro area grew to over 231,619 (CARA 1996a), an increase of 110 percent in just six years. Of these, 9,571 (4 percent) are children in school (CARA 1996a). This growth has changed the cultural makeup of the city: a Mexican owns three radio stations that broadcast in Spanish, and in 1997 there were three Spanish language newspapers, one of them owned by a Mexican. By 1999, there were eleven such papers. Mexican workers play an important role in the service sector, as well as in construction and industry. Meatpacking concerns, especially chicken-processing plants, must be located close to farms to reduce losses of live animals in transportation. Packers are therefore tied to the production region, although they use up the local work force because of the arduous and dangerous working conditions, as well as low salaries. Once the native work force has been used up, new sources of workers (women, African Americans, migrants) are recruited (Saindon 1991).

This recent increase in the number of Hispanics in the southeastern United States indicates that there is a specific demand for their labor. This demand is due in part to construction associated with the 1996 Olympic games, but that event does not explain the increase that began even before Atlanta was selected as the host city. Other changes in the labor market, such as the increased demand for carpet and textile factory workers and for domestics, gardeners, and restaurant workers, have played a part.

Atlanta is a secondary U.S. destination for most Mexican male migrants, who come to the city from elsewhere. On average, men migrate the year after they marry, whereas women on average migrate four years after marriage. About 10 percent of female migrants are single. Women typically start working informally in child care for other Mexicans (at a typical rate of $10 per day per child). Then they can move into domestic service or hotel work. One woman who was interviewed cleaned houses; when asked if she wanted to get another job, she replied, "I can't because I don't have working papers." But her daughters have found jobs in hotels (Nettles 1997).

Most women follow their spouses. "Few women come alone; most come once their husband has gotten settled. It's a terrible life without their wives," according to one of my informants, a priest who works at the Misión Católica. Juan is a young man who has been in Atlanta for a few years working in carpet installation. Telling me about his wife, who is still in Mexico, he says, "She is very sharp, she organizes informal credit groups and gets a commission. She sells tamales, corn on the cob, pigs, and chickens. I'm going to bring her up here. Most of the men bring their wives now."

Since the 1990s, most women migrants from Mexico follow their husbands to Atlanta within three years of the males' migration. I found no women who had come to Atlanta before 1980, and most arrived after 1990. Because of the lack of official data on Mexican immigrants, I relied on a combination of official data for the overall population and inferences from ethnographic interviews to estimate the number of Mexican women in Atlanta.

THE NUMBERS

I found many more women than I expected; at Catholic Mass, for example, more than half of those in attendance were women (compared, however, with 90 percent of those attending churches in Mexico). I found many women working in restaurants, domestic service, meat-packing companies, carpet factories, hotel service, and religious services. We surveyed forty-nine women at three sites in Atlanta in the spring of 1998 with a simple instrument that asked about family, migration history, household composition, and expenses. We have no official data about the number of Mexican women in Atlanta, but there are more than 9,571 children in the public schools whose first language is Spanish (CARA 1996a). If we calculate that 80 percent of them are Mexican, we have 7,656 Mexican children. How many women does each child represent?

Extrapolating from the numbers of preschool, school-age, and adult children reported by women in our 1998 survey (Rees, Miller, and Arillo 1998), we concluded that there are approximately 12,785 Mexican women in the metropolitan area, more than three times the number of our pre-survey estimate of 3,500.

One of the problems with the survey data is that they may overestimate the number of children in school. Many Mexican children drop out between the tenth and eleventh grades. In addition, some of the women have left older children in Mexico. Because our survey was carried out in social service agencies, it may be biased toward working-class migrants, although all groups of Mexicans come to the Mexican Consulate, one of our sites. Adding in a 10 percent overcalculation factor, I conclude that there were least 11,500 Mexican women in Atlanta in early 1999. It should be obvious that given the rapid growth in the number of Mexicans overall in Atlanta, this number has long since been surpassed.

DISCUSSION

Meillassoux (1981), commenting on social reproduction theory, holds that women and children migrate only if the husband's salary is enough to support the whole family at the destination location. Our data from Atlanta permit us to reject this scenario. Most Mexican men earn more than the minimum wage ($6 per hour is common), but the net income is less than $800 per month. Even with overtime or second jobs, the income is around $1,200, not enough to support a family of four or five. Reported monthly expenses come to at least $500 per adult ($200 for rent and utilities, $200 for food, $100 for clothes); a man can send $500 home to Mexico, but he cannot support his family in the United States on what he alone earns. Mean monthly expenses for a family of four with one worker are at least $1,400, which is $200 more than the average male income. In order to support a family in Atlanta, a household needs more than one wage earner. Since there is a specific demand for female labor (Massey et al. 1994), it is possible for the women to contribute to the household income.

Among Mexican migrants to Los Angeles, it is becoming more common for the women to join their husbands earlier in their marriages (Hondagneu-Sotelo 1994:103). The Atlanta data indicate that families follow men shortly after they get settled in the United States, but this trend appears to apply only to younger households. Of households formed before 1970, only 50 percent of the wives migrated, and they did so long after (up to fifteen years later) their husbands. Among the younger families, women follow their husbands after an average of only three years.

The number of Mexican women in the United States in general and in Atlanta in particular is increasing rapidly. If our estimate of about

11,500 for 1999 is even roughly correct, then Mexican women are still a small portion of the Mexican population of over 185,000 (80 percent of the total Hispanic population). But in the absence of official figures, we must remember that women are systematically undercounted. In addition, Mexicans and U.S.-born Hispanics are lumped in with other Spanish-speaking immigrants. Because of this undercount, the most reliable source of data is the count of Spanish-speaking children in the public schools, but even this source has been eliminated as of 1996, when schools were no longer required to collect and report such figures.

The presence of Mexican women in Atlanta obviously affects the Mexican community, social services, employment, and culture. These trends will increase in salience as numbers continue to grow. The official avoidance of accurate counting only makes it more difficult to understand and attend to this population.

NOTES

A previous version of this paper was presented at the annual meetings of the Southern Anthropological Society, Decatur, Georgia, in February 1999.

1. Interviews were conducted by the author, and by T. Danyael Miller and Mariposa Arillo, who were research scholars at Agnes Scott College at the time.

2. For some reason, the censuses do not differentiate by country of origin or ethnicity when it comes to Spanish speakers, which causes multiple confusion: white and black Cubans and people born in the United States whose first language is Spanish (regardless of specific ethnicity) are all classified as "Hispanic."

REFERENCES

Bustamante, J., C. Reynolds, and R. Hinojosa Ojeda. 1992. *U.S.-Mexico Relations: Labor Market Interdependences*. Stanford: Stanford University Press.

Castells, M. 1980. *The Economic Crisis and American Society*. Princeton, N.J.: Princeton University Press.

Center for Applied Research in Anthropology (CARA). 1996a. *Georgia Hispanic Population, 1981–1995*. Atlanta: CARA.

———. 1996b. *Metro Atlanta Immigrants*. Atlanta: CARA.

Collins, J. 1988. *Unseasonal Migrations: The Effects of Rural Labor Scarcity in Peru*. Princeton, N.J.: Princeton University Press.

Cornelius, W. 1991. Los Migrantes de la Crisis: The Changing Profile of Mexican Migration to the U.S. In *Social Responses to Mexico's Economic Crisis of the 1980s*, ed. M. González de la Rocha and A. Escobar Latapi, 155–92. San Diego: University of California Center for U.S.-Mexican Studies.

Donato, K. 1992. Current Trends and Patterns of Female Migration: Evidence from Mexico. *International Migration Review* 27(4):748–71.

Hondagneu-Sotelo, P. 1994. *Gendered Transitions: Mexican Experiences of Immigration*. Berkeley: University of California Press.

Instituto Nacional de Estadística Geografía e Informática (INEGI). 1992. Anuario Estadístico de los Estados Unidos Mexicanos, Edición 1990. México: Secretaría de Programación y Presupuesto.

Jenkins, J. 1977. Push/Pull in Recent Mexican Migration to the U.S. *International Migration Review* 11:178–89.

Luque González, R., and R. Corona Cuapio. 1992. La Migración y la Dinámica Demográfica de Oaxaca. In *Migración y Etnicidad en Oaxaca*, ed. J. Corbett, 13–18. Nashville: Vanderbilt Publications in Anthropology, Vanderbilt University.

Massey, D., J. Arango, G. Hugo, A. Kouaouci, A. Pellegrino, and J. Taylor. 1994. An Evaluation of International Migration Theory: The North American Case. *Population and Development Review* 20(4):699–751.

Meillassoux, C. 1981. *Maidens, Meal, and Money*. Cambridge: Cambridge University Press.

Nettles, J. 1997. Desde Muy Lejos: Un Estudio de la Vida de una Mujer Inmigrante, Mexicana. Senior research paper, Agnes Scott College.

Pedraza-Bailey, S. 1985. *Political and Economic Migrants in America: Cubans and Mexicans*. Austin: University of Texas Press.

Rees, M. 1998. Women Managing Migration: Household and Agriculture in Oaxaca. Paper presented at the annual meetings of the American Anthropological Association, Washington, D.C., 21–24 November.

Rees, M., T. Miller, and M. Arillo. 1998. *Atlanta Latinas*. Atlanta: Center for Latin American and Hispanic Studies.

Saindon, J. 1991. *Piney Road: Work Education and the Remaking of the Southern Family*. Washington, D.C.: Ford Foundation.

Stephen, L. 1990. *Zapotec Women*. Austin: University of Texas Press.

Stier, H., and M. Tienda. 1992. Family, Work, and Women: The Labor Supply of Hispanic Immigrant Wives. *International Migration Review* 26(4):1291–313.

Woo-Morales, O. 1995. Las Mujeres Mexicanas Indocumentadas en la Migración Internacional y la Movilidad Transfronteriza. In *Mujeres, Migración y Maquila en la Frontera Norte*, ed. S. Loaeza, O. Ruiz, L. Velaxco, and O. Woo-Morales, 78–98. Tijuana: El Colegio de México y El Colegio de la Frontera Norte.

Industry and Immigration in Dalton, Georgia

James D. Engstrom

In the current period of economic restructuring, immigrants from Latin America and Asia account for an increasing proportion of the industrial labor force in the United States. The participation of these new immigrants in industrial labor markets is viewed as a largely urban phenomenon and is often studied within an urban context (Portes and Stepick 1993; Waldinger 1986; Waldinger and Bozorgmehr 1996); nevertheless, a less visible transformation is taking place in many smaller cities and towns across the United States as industries ranging from food processing to textiles are employing immigrant workers in growing numbers (Broadway 1994; Cravey 1997; McCurry 1998; Poole 1998).

One place where the impact of the new immigration is evident is Dalton, Georgia, a small manufacturing city that produces more than half of all the carpet in the United States. Faced with a tight labor market, Dalton's carpet manufacturers have welcomed increasing numbers of Mexican immigrants over the last decade. Dalton's carpet executives credit Mexican immigrants with helping the industry survive and grow ("Rural Communities" 1998; England 1998; Maggs 1998; Rozelle 1998). Local industrialists are highly supportive of the recent immigration, but local political leaders have been forced to negotiate between the manufacturers' positive portrayal of the immigrants and the more ambivalent attitudes held by others in the community.

The recent immigration of Mexicans to Dalton provides an excellent opportunity to examine the interconnections among immigrants, industry, labor markets, and place. As I trace Dalton's rise as a local industrial district dedicated to carpet production, I examine the labor market dynamics that have characterized the industry, including claims of chronic labor shortages, and the dramatic growth of the Mexican immigrant work force since the mid-1980s. I explore the unforeseen demographic changes in Dalton resulting from the Mexican migration and the contradictory positions of Dalton's political leaders as they try to respond to the competing claims of residents and industrialists. I conclude with a brief examination of efforts concerning education and illegal immigration started in response to the community's demographic transformation.

INDUSTRIAL DISTRICTS AS SOCIO-SPATIAL FORMATIONS

We can comprehend Dalton's evolution into the "Carpet Capital of the World" by viewing the community as a socio-spatial formation of the type known as an industrial district. Industrial districts are composed of highly concentrated clusters of similar industries that draw on external benefits in the local environment, including a specialized labor force and the growth of subsidiary industries providing raw materials, machinery, and product distribution. Opportunities for frequent face-to-face communications within the district foster innovations and product improvements (Sunley 1992). Contemporary scholars focus on industrial districts as geographically embedded social systems supported by a variety of institutions and norms of behavior (Saxenian 1990; Scott 1988). A spirit of trust and cooperative competition characterizes successful districts, where companies share information and work together on common problems (Lorenz 1992; Piore and Sabel 1984). Local social institutions, ranging from educational systems to labor unions, support the industrial sector and help reproduce local labor markets (Peck 1996). Firms often work collectively to influence local social environments and institutions in ways that benefit the dominant industry (Jonas 1992; Saxenian 1989). Companies broaden their influence by participating in public-private coalitions called *urban regimes*, which enable them to develop a capacity to act through shared interests and long-standing personal relations (Stone 1993).

Northwest Georgia's carpet manufacturing district, with Dalton at its center, emerged during the twentieth century from the local development of a new process for producing carpets. This process, tufting, involves threading fabric through a backing material; it was an almost extinct handicraft tradition that was revived in the Dalton area around

1900. Beginning as a cottage industry involving the hand-tufting of bed-spreads, the industry had moved into factories by the late 1920s (Deaton 1993). New Deal wage legislation increased the labor costs of producing bedspreads, stimulating innovations in tufting machinery. Tufting machines got bigger, and by the 1950s, textile machinery companies in Dalton and nearby Chattanooga were making machines as wide as twelve feet across; such machines, which could produce single pieces of wall-to-wall carpet, became the foundation of the modern tufted carpet industry (Deaton 1993).

Entrepreneurs in Dalton started new carpet-manufacturing companies, and others moved to the area to establish businesses. The new tufted industry caught the tradition-bound woven carpet industry by surprise. Tufted carpet was less expensive than woven carpet because the process was easy to learn and used less labor (Toyne et al. 1983). With the post–World War II housing boom and changing consumer tastes, the national market for tufted carpet exploded. In 1951 only 9 percent of all carpets sold in the United States were tufted. By 1968, tufted carpet accounted for 90 percent of all carpets sold in the country (Kirk 1970).

With the rise of the local tufted carpet industry, dozens of specialized firms providing materials, dyeing and finishing services, machinery, and wholesaling services sprang up nearby. Fueled by continuous local innovation and growing demand, the industry grew rapidly and began to require a larger labor force. A few carpet manufacturers opened plants elsewhere in the southeastern states, but most companies chose to remain in Dalton, where they could more easily maintain ongoing relationships with machinery makers, suppliers, and distributors.

THE CHRONIC LABOR SHORTAGE

Carpet manufacturers benefited by locating in Dalton, but they faced substantial challenges when it came to finding workers. The tufted carpet industry grew so rapidly that residents from Dalton and surrounding Whitfield County could not fill all of the industry's labor needs. Workers began commuting from as far as fifty miles away to work in Dalton's factories. The demand for labor pushed wages higher than in most other subsectors of the textile industry. Even so, workers remained a relative bargain; in 1987 the manufacturing wage in Whitfield County was 83.5 percent of the national average (U.S. Department of Commerce 1987).

By the mid-1960s, Dalton's carpet manufacturers were complaining publicly about labor shortages. Executives grumbled about the inability to retain workers in a labor market in which dissatisfied employees could quit their jobs at one firm and immediately find employment at another (Plice 1976). Company owners also mentioned the difficulty of finding workers for second and third shifts, which they had instituted to keep up with growing demand. These complaints were interrupted only during a few brief periods of recession, and they reached a fever pitch by the mid-1980s (Burritt 1987).

Available data provide some support for the manufacturers' claims. During the 1960s, unemployment rates in Whitfield County were actually higher than those in Georgia and the country as a whole, although they rarely exceeded 5 percent. During the 1970s and early 1980s, however, unemployment rates were lower than U.S. and Georgia rates, except during the recessionary periods of 1974–76 and 1980–82. Since the mid-1980s, the county's unemployment rate has remained consistently below state and national levels. The healthy U.S. economy of the mid-1990s fueled demand for consumer durables, and Whitfield County's unemployment rate fell to an all-time low of 2.9 percent in 1998 (Georgia Department of Labor 1999). Commuting patterns also show that few local residents had to leave Whitfield County to find work. According to census data, only 11 percent of workers in the county commuted to another county for work in 1970; that figure fell to 9.8 percent in 1990. On the other hand, rates of out-of-county commuting rose elsewhere in the United States from 17.8 percent to 23.9 percent during those same years (U.S. Bureau of the Census 1970, 1990).

Regardless of whether these statistics paint a compelling portrait of a labor shortage, the consistent complaints of the industry reflected a commonly held perception that workers were hard to find and keep. Under such conditions, one might surmise that Dalton's carpet companies would locate plants in other places where labor markets were not so competitive. Most carpet companies remained in Dalton, however, and some even consolidated their operations in the area. The positive aspects of being in a specialized industrial district apparently outweighed the negative effects of a labor shortage. Moreover, as the industry became more highly concentrated after a series of buyouts, Dalton-based firms emerged as the strongest companies. The place-based capitalists who owned these companies positioned themselves not only as key players in the economic arena but also as "good corporate citizens," strongly committed to the community and its local institutions (Engstrom 1998). It is clear that a local solution to the labor shortage was preferred by most of Dalton's carpet companies.

MEXICAN IMMIGRATION TO DALTON

During the 1970s, the growing chicken-processing industry in northern Georgia was attracting Mexican workers, and some came to work in Dalton's large chicken-processing plant. More migrants moved to the area from Texas during the early 1980s as that state's construction boom ended (Williams 1998). By the mid-1980s, the Mexican community in Dalton had grown to an estimated 2,000 people, and immigrants were increasingly finding work in the carpet mills (Galloway 1986). With continued global restructuring and the ongoing decline of Mexico's agricultural sector, Mexicans increased their dependence on migration to the United States during the 1990s (Massey, Goldring, and Durand 1994). This restructuring had a local impact in Dalton, where migration increased dramatically throughout the decade.

Migrants to Dalton found ample employment opportunities in the carpet factories. In any given year over the last decade, more than 120 carpet establishments in Whitfield County employed more than 15,000 workers (U.S. Department of Commerce 1998). Carpet manufacturers claimed that technological changes in the industry created the need for workers with a high school education and computer literacy, but many mill jobs apparently still did not require either of those credentials or even the ability to speak English. As more Mexicans migrated to Dalton, they concentrated in blue-collar industries. According to the U.S. Bureau of the Census (1999), 69.7 percent of the 1,183 Hispanic workers in the county were employed in blue-collar industrial occupations in 1990, compared with 55 percent of the African Americans and 42.5 percent for the whites.

The officially reported number of Hispanics in Whitfield County in 1990 was not, however, very large. According to the U.S. Bureau of the Census (1990), only 1,183 of the 37,649 employees in Whitfield County (or 3.1 percent of the total work force) were Hispanic. Hispanics accounted for only 3.2 percent of the total county population of 72,462. The pace of Mexican migration to Dalton appears to have picked up considerably in the 1990s, however, as it has in many other parts of the southeastern states (Williams 1998). Current estimates of the Hispanic population in the Dalton area (more than 90 percent of which is Mexican) vary widely. The 1997 U.S. census estimate is 4,581, about 5.6 percent of the total population of Whitfield County (U.S. Bureau of the Census 1999). On the other hand, the Immigration and Naturalization Service estimated that almost 40,000 Hispanics were living in the area in 1997 ("Rural Communities" 1998).

School attendance figures provide one solid source of data for measuring incremental change in the area's Mexican population. Whitfield County has two school systems, the smaller city of Dalton system and the larger Whitfield County system, which serves all residents of the county living outside Dalton's corporate limits. The Dalton system shows a dramatic rise in the percentage of Hispanic students, from 4 percent in 1989 to 21 percent in 1995 to 42 percent in 1998. The Dalton system enrolled 911 Hispanic students in 1993, and by 1998 the Hispanic enrollment had grown to 2,027 students. Even more dramatic, two of Dalton's six elementary schools reached more than 70 percent Hispanic enrollment by 1998 (Georgia Department of Education 1999). The enrollment data for the county system are not as dramatic but also show a substantial increase in the number of Hispanic students. In 1994, there were 406 Hispanic students in the county system (3.9 percent of the total enrollment), and by 1998 this number had risen to 1,182 (10.7 percent of the total). The school data provide solid evidence for the rapid increase in the number of Mexicans in Dalton and Whitfield County, but the total numbers and percentages of Hispanics will likely be open to interpretation for some time to come. It is unlikely that the 2000 census will bring closure to the question, although it will certainly provide a new set of numbers over which to argue.

IMMIGRANTS AND LABOR MARKETS

A large body of literature on labor market segmentation demonstrates that some industries prefer to hire immigrant labor. Employers often perceive immigrants to be hardworking and loyal, willing to work for lower wages, and less likely to complain about working conditions than native-born workers. In large cities such as New York and Los Angeles, immigrants have found employment in apparel, toy, and footwear industries, enabling those industries to reduce labor costs and remain competitive in an increasingly international market. Away from the great metropolitan areas, however, the transformation to a foreign-born work force has begun in the meatpacking industry in the western Great Plains, in the poultry-processing industry in the South, and most recently in the southern textile industry (McCurry 1998).

In Dalton, a special set of factors precipitated the increased demand for labor. Dalton's economy has not been diversifying; it has continued to focus almost completely on the carpet industry. Unlike other subsectors of the textile industry, carpet manufacturing has remained healthy over the last thirty years, even as it has consolidated into fewer and larger firms. Dalton has not aggressively sought new industry, and the carpet industry has discouraged large employers that might take "their" workers away from Dalton. The labor market in Dalton is in many ways held captive by the carpet industry. Nevertheless, even this captive labor market has been unable to generate the number of workers needed in the local factories.

When Mexican immigrants began arriving in the offices of the carpet mills looking for work, the manufacturers were not in a position to turn them away. The industry executives very quickly began to speak highly of the work ethic of the new immigrants (Engstrom 1998). Manufacturers throughout the country routinely praise the industriousness and tirelessness of Mexican immigrants, and in that sense Dalton's industrialists were not unusual. What is dramatic in Dalton, however, is how quickly the discourse about hard work and loyalty switched from one ethnic group to another. Since the rise of the carpet industry in the 1950s, carpet manufacturers have sung the praises of native-born workers from Appalachia, but Dalton's corporate executives are now referring to the Mexicans as a "godsend" and the "lifeblood" of the industry (England 1998; Rozelle 1998).

IMMIGRATION, COMMUNITY CONFLICT, AND CHANGE

Dalton's industrialists probably underestimated the magnitude of the transformation that would take place in the community as the numbers of Mexican workers grew. Mexican immigrants began to alter this quiet Appalachian community by finding housing in particular neighborhoods, opening businesses catering to Mexican customers, enrolling their chil-

dren in local schools, and bringing with them religious and leisure practices that stood out from those of the long-term residents. Three Spanish-language newspapers and a Spanish radio station opened to serve
northwest Georgia's rapidly growing Mexican community. Attendance
skyrocketed at Dalton's only Catholic church, where services are now
mostly conducted in Spanish. A second Catholic church has been
planned, spurred by a large donation from one of Dalton's carpet manufacturers (Rozelle 1998). Another carpet executive orchestrated the
donation of private land and helped raise one million dollars for the
construction of a soccer complex used primarily by Mexican families
(England 1998). These efforts echo activities carried out a few decades
earlier when carpet manufacturers helped to establish softball diamonds
throughout the community for its Anglo work force.

With the increasing visibility of Mexican immigrants in the factories, schools, and neighborhoods, however, the carpet industry became
a target of criticism from some long-term residents. This criticism was
the first significant challenge by residents to the industry's assertions
that what was good for the industry was good for the community. Local residents rarely criticized the industry in public, and the manufacturers viewed themselves (and were viewed by many residents) as be-
nevolent capitalists responsible for Dalton's economic good fortune and
as good corporate citizens committed to building strong local institutions. Dalton's carpet industry enjoyed a local hegemony that stifled
public debate. Almost every person in town worked for the industry or
one of its subsidiaries, or had a family member who did so. Most residents understood that Dalton's social contract involved identification
with or acquiescence to the needs of the industry.

The local carpet industry actively participated in Dalton's urban regime. The industry and other community leaders usually spoke as one
collective voice and tried to keep internal dissent out of view. Because
local political leaders recognized the economic influence of the industry, they also usually supported the industry's actions and positions on
community issues. In Dalton, political debate was closely circumscribed.

The migration of Mexicans to Dalton, however, seemed to open up
possibilities for political debate. Accusations that carpet companies
knowingly hired illegal workers became more frequent. Some Dalton
residents suggested that carpet company representatives traveled to
Mexico to recruit laborers, and others claimed that Mexican immigrants

were taking jobs away from long-term residents. Some people demanded public meetings to discuss illegal immigration, and letters to the editor appeared in the local newspaper complaining that the new migrants were not interested in being "American" and that they did not pay taxes to support city and county services being provided to them.

Industry leaders were quick to defend themselves and the new migrants. Many executives insisted that Mexicans brought documentation when they applied for jobs, although it was beyond the capabilities of the companies to prove whether the documents were legitimate. They also stated that because of the labor shortage, Mexican immigrants were not taking jobs away from anyone but instead were taking jobs that would otherwise have remained unfilled. Carpet manufacturers insisted that the new workers were essential to continued profitability of the industry, pointing out that the health of the community depended on the success of the industry.

While the industry maintained its defensive posture, local political leaders began to feel pressure to respond to growing concerns about the impact of immigration. They tried to deflect the more racist sentiments of some residents but felt compelled to act regarding the issue of illegal immigration. As participants in the urban regime, political leaders continued to espouse the dominant discourse about the positive contributions of Mexican immigrants to the industry and, by extension, to the community. In response to citizen concerns, however, the elected officials of Dalton and Whitfield County established a Commission on Immigration, consisting mainly of local officials and law enforcement authorities (Turner-Collins 1995). At first, the local business community kept its distance from this commission, adopting a wait-and-see attitude. The commission's final recommendations, which revolved around greater cooperation among law enforcement agencies and developing technology to enable companies to identify illegal immigrants, were eventually endorsed by the Dalton-Whitfield Chamber of Commerce, many of whose members were carpet companies (Dalton-Whitfield Chamber of Commerce 1995).

Another action resulting from the recommendations of the Commission on Immigration was the establishment of a task force that operated as an informal extension of the Immigration and Naturalization Service (INS). Many residents wanted the INS to open an office in

Dalton but were informed that there were not enough resources to do so. In order to demonstrate that they were serious about reducing illegal immigration, however, the city and county governments jointly contributed a total of $100,000 to operate the task force office, which was staffed by local law enforcement officers, who had no authority to detain people on questions related to residency. INS officials visited the office at least three times a week and considered this blended city-county-federal initiative a possible model for future cooperation between local communities and the INS (Turner-Collins 1995). Although some residents applauded the opening of the task force office, others saw it as a symbolic gesture, rather than as a substantive effort to crack down on illegal immigration.

Another point of community conflict emerged in the school systems. The rapid increase of Hispanic students caught the public schools by surprise. The two systems had only minimal capabilities for addressing the needs of Spanish-speaking students. Long-term residents complained that the education of English-speaking students was being neglected, and some white parents began to withdraw their children from the public schools (Dyer 1999; Maggs 1998). Spanish-speaking students were also becoming frustrated, and many dropped out of high school.

The carpet industry began to search for solutions to this education crisis. Using personal networks that grew out of a joint venture in Mexico, Dalton's largest carpet company helped to arrange an exchange program between the Dalton system and a Mexican university, which now has several of its graduates working as teachers' aides in local schools (Maggs 1998). The exchange program is funded primarily by the local school systems, but it also has financial support from the industry, exemplifying the public-private collective action that is so pervasive in Dalton. The community still struggles with educational issues, since Hispanic students without legal immigrant status do not have access to opportunities for higher education. Many Mexican students find themselves in a bind, seeing no possible future but to drop out of high school to work in the mills, as their Anglo predecessors had done twenty years before (Dyer 1999).

It is worth noting that the carpet industry, a loud and respected voice in the community, is publicly articulating a positive response to immigration and is celebrating the new multiculturalism of Dalton. Moreover, Dalton's political leaders have largely avoided the punitive policy measures that some other government jurisdictions have directed against immigrants. These circumstances suggest that peaceful coexistence and mutual respect between Anglos and Hispanics may be achievable in Dalton. In supporting its new immigrant work force, however, the carpet industry may have contributed to a dynamic process over which it ultimately can exert little control. The industry still may control the work force, but its tight grasp on the community may have loosened as its decades-old hegemony has come under some public scrutiny. A multicultural Dalton may open up the possibility that multiple voices, and not just those of the carpet industry, can speak and that a more inclusive and democratic local political dialogue can emerge.

REFERENCES

Broadway, M. 1994. Beef Stew: Cattle, Immigrants, and Established Residents in a Kansas Beefpacking Town. In *Newcomers in the Workplace: Immigrants and the Restructuring of the U.S. Economy*, ed. L. Lamphere, A. Stepick, and G. Grenier, 2–43. Philadelphia: Temple University Press.

Burritt, C. 1987. Labor Shortage in Northwest Georgia: Carpet Mills Can't Hire Enough Workers for Growing Demand. *Atlanta Journal and Constitution*, August 24, D1, 8.

Cravey, A. 1997. Latino Labor and Poultry Production in Rural North Carolina. *Southeastern Geographer* 37:295–300.

Dalton-Whitfield Chamber of Commerce. 1995. Chamber Endorses Work of Joint Immigration Task Force. *Link* 15:11.

Deaton, T. 1993. *Bedspreads to Broadlooms: The Story of the Tufted Carpet Industry*. Chattanooga: Color Wheel.

Dyer, J. 1999. The Dreams of Rigo Nuñez. *Atlanta Journal and Constitution*, January 24, C1, 4–5.

England, T. 1998. Jobs, Jobs, Jobs! *Time*, January 28, 61–63.

Engstrom, J. 1998. Industry, Social Regulation, and Scale: The Carpet Manufacturing Complex of Dalton, Georgia. Ph.D. diss., Clark University.

Galloway, J. 1986. Dalton's Jobs Attracting Illegal Aliens: Textile Industry Center with Low Unemployment Feeling Impact of Growing Mexican Community. *Atlanta Journal and Constitution*, August 26, A12.

Georgia Department of Education. 1999. *Student Enrollment Reports*. http://www.doe.k12.ga.us (last accessed on June 10, 2000).

Georgia Department of Labor. 1999. *Annual Unemployment Averages*. Atlanta: Georgia Department of Labor.

Jonas, A. 1992. Corporate Takeover and the Politics of Community: The Case of Norton Company in Worcester. *Economic Geography* 68:348–72.

Kirk, R. 1970. *The Carpet Industry: Present Status and Future Prospects.* Philadelphia: University of Pennsylvania Press.

Lorenz, E. 1992. Trust, Community, and Cooperation: Toward a Theory of Industrial Districts. In *Pathways to Industrialization and Regional Development,* ed. M. Storper and A. Scott, 195–204. London: Routledge.

Maggs, J. 1998. Turning to Mexico for Help. *National Journal* 30(50):2945–46.

Massey, D., J. Goldring, and J. Durand. 1994. Continuity in Transnational Migration: An Analysis of Nineteen Mexican Communities. *American Journal of Sociology* 99:1492–1533.

McCurry, J. 1998. Textile Firms Face Tight Labor Pool. *Textile World* 148:22.

Peck, J. 1996. *Work-Place: The Social Regulation of Labor Markets.* New York: Guilford.

Piore, M., and C. Sabel. 1984. *The Second Industrial Divide.* New York: Basic Books.

Plice, S. 1976. *Manpower and Merger: The Impact of Merger upon Personnel Policies in the Carpet and Furniture Industries.* Philadelphia: University of Pennsylvania Press.

Poole, S. 1998. Southern Economic Survey: The Latin Influence. *Atlanta Journal and Constitution,* April 19, P4.

Portes, A., and A. Stepick. 1993. *City on the Edge: The Transformation of Miami.* Berkeley: University of California Press.

Rozelle, W. 1998. Hispanics: Lifeblood of Dalton's Carpet Workforce. *Textile World* 148:85–87.

Rural Communities: Southeast Hispanics, Tobacco. 1998. *Rural Migration News* 4:1–2.

Saxenian, A. 1989. In Search of Power: The Organization of Business Interests in Silicon Valley. *Economy and Society* 18:25–70.

———. 1990. Regional Networks and the Resurgence of Silicon Valley. *California Management Review* 33:89–112.

Scott, A. 1988. *New Industrial Spaces: Flexible Production Organization and Regional Development in North America and Western Europe.* London: Pion.

Stone, C. 1993. Urban Regimes and the Capacity to Govern: A Political Economy Approach. *Journal of Urban Affairs* 15:1–28.

Sunley, P. 1992. Marshallian Industrial Districts: The Case of the Lancashire Cotton Industry in the Inter-war Years. *Transactions, Institute of British Geographers* 17:306–20.

Toyne, B., J. Arpan, A. Barnett, D. Ricks, T. Shimp, J. Andrews, J. Clamp, C. Rogers, G. Shepherd, T. Tho, E. Vaughn, and S. Woolcock. 1983. *The U.S.*

Textile Mill Products Industry: Strategies for the 1980s and Beyond. Columbia: University of South Carolina Press.

Turner-Collins, R. 1995. Task Force Funding Has Green Light. *Dalton Daily Citizen News*, July 19, 1A, 3A.

U.S. Bureau of the Census. 1970. *Census of Population.* Washington, D.C.: Government Printing Office.

———. 1990. *Census of Population.* Washington, D.C.: Government Printing Office.

———. 1999. *Population Estimates for Counties by Race and Hispanic Origin.* http://www.census.gov/population/estimates/county/crh/crhga97.txt (last accessed on June 10, 2000).

U.S. Department of Commerce. 1987. *Census of Manufacturers.* Washington, D.C.: Government Printing Office.

———. 1998. *County Business Patterns.* Washington, D.C.: Government Printing Office.

Waldinger, R. 1986. *Through the Eye of the Needle: Immigrants and Enterprise in New York's Garment Trades.* New York: New York University Press.

Waldinger, R., and M. Bozorgmehr, eds. 1996. *Ethnic Los Angeles.* New York: Russell Sage Foundation.

Williams, M. 1998. Special Economic Report: Not on Easy Street—Migrants Face Big Obstacles as They Search for Better Life in the U.S. *Atlanta Journal and Constitution*, April 19, P3.

Mexican Places in Southern Spaces: Globalization, Work, and Daily Life in and around the North Georgia Poultry Industry

Greig Guthey

Down the street from the water tower emblazoned with the words "Poultry Capital of the World," past the trucks, chickens, and windblown feathers at two chicken-processing plants in Gainesville, Georgia, is a small enclave of Mexican businesses where one can purchase food that is not available in mainstream supermarkets, or step up to a *taquería* (taco stand) for an authentic Mexican meal, and seldom hear English spoken.[1] In the surrounding region, there are churches of all kinds holding Spanish-language services and perhaps evening English-language classes as well. Regular bus service leaves Gainesville for Mexico. On weekends, Latino soccer teams may be seen playing on local athletic fields. Just southwest of Gainesville is Forsyth County; census figures from 1997 indicate that the county's population includes some 2,000 Hispanics, a noteworthy figure in light of the fact that the population includes only 39 blacks and that the county is considered the whitest, as well as the fastest-growing, in the country (Firestone 1999). There are places with similarly growing Hispanic populations in Athens, Chamblee, and other communities in North Georgia.

Many of the Hispanic people work in poultry-processing plants in the region. Indeed, there is a strong relationship between that industry and Mexican migration (Griffith 1993; Katz 1996; Stull, Broadway, and Griffith 1995; Walker 1989). Much of the literature, however, examines the ways in which industries construct new labor markets through immigrant social networks. This approach has added to our understanding of the dynamics of the poultry- and meat-processing industries generally, but the most widely cited studies tend to portray immigrants as

subjects of industry manipulation or as refugees from economic distur-
bances in their sending countries. Moreover, workers in these accounts
appear either as short-term sojourners, as farm workers using poultry-
processing employment only during the off-season, or as a new class
of exploited workers. I take a different view. In order to flesh out the
story of immigrants in North Georgia, I used a snowball sampling
method to interview twenty-two immigrant workers about what they
have done since their arrival. I find that in more than two decades, the
situation of these immigrants has changed; they have become more
stable and stand to have long-term influences on the rural areas in which
they live.

SETTLING IN

An important element in the dynamic affecting the poultry industry,
North Georgia, and Mexican workers is the possibility that residence
in the United States allows immigrants to bring family members to the
state to benefit from local educational institutions. The immigrants tend
to see their situation in terms of upward mobility, not in terms of exploitation. For example, many of the businesses serving the immigrant
community in Gainesville were started by the immigrants themselves.
One of my sources, a reporter for a Spanish-language tabloid who is
herself an immigrant from Peru, boasted that Hispanics are the world's
best entrepreneurs. Her view was shared by others I interviewed. "There
are a lot of people like me," commented a restaurant owner who worked
in the poultry plants for five years before starting his own business. His
restaurant includes a lunch truck that makes rounds to the plants during breaks. "We're making our lives here," he said.

The immigrants' choice of location does, however, have some negative aspects. While they may be making their lives here in the economic
sense, they still experience an emotional pull toward Mexico and its way
of life. The restaurant owner explained, "It's a better life there [in
Mexico]. Not in an economic way, but the people live more happily there.
They live more slowly. You're not in a rush. People have time to go to
the street and talk. Somebody in the U.S., you don't even have time to
know who your neighbor is." A twenty-nine-year-old cook agreed, explaining that life in the United States was *sin sabor* (flavorless).

Although life in Mexico may be preferable in general terms, the immigrants have developed social networks in the United States to the extent that many now question whether they will ever return to their hometowns on a permanent basis. Many of these workers feel tied to North Georgia because their children are enrolled in local schools. An immigrant who has been working in the plants for seven years explained, "I think I am going to save money and go back to Mexico. [But] my kids are in school now. I think I will go back to Mexico, but you never know." The restaurant owner had returned to Mexico only once in twelve years, and in that time he had acquired some southern dialect: "I'm fixin' to go back, but I have three kids and I want them to go to school and go to college. But I'd like to die in Mexico." A thirty-two-year-old woman with two children explained, "In Mexico, there is nothing. There is nothing to eat. There is nothing to live on. I want to return to Mexico. But we don't have anything in Mexico. Here at least there is work."

In contrast to previous research, which emphasized the cyclical nature of migration in the area, my study suggests that the immigrants are now a stable presence in the area. Many of the workers insisted that, sentiment aside, they were not inclined to go back to Mexico unless forced to do so by the Immigration and Naturalization Service. "We like it here because we have everything we want," said one woman. Another woman, who had been in the country for fourteen months, added, "For the moment, [chicken processing] is the best job possible," although she hoped to return to Mexico after one additional year. When I asked a twenty-five-year-old worker whether he intended to go back, he said, "Maybe yes, maybe no. Maybe if the government changes. They only do what the biggest, richest Mexicans want." Expressions of dissatisfaction with the Mexican government were common in my interviews.

INDUSTRY WORKER AND WORKER INDUSTRY INFLUENCES

In addition to educational and financial opportunities, the immigrants cite emerging relationships between the poultry industry and its workers as an important factor in their willingness to stay in the area. The managers I interviewed told of changing employment policies that allowed them to decrease their turnover rates. One plant had instituted drug testing as a condition for employment, and turnover had decreased as a result. Another plant had changed its vacation policy, the better to accommodate workers' schedules. The old system of one-week vacations has given way to a policy allowing for a week of unpaid leave of absence after one year's tenure so that workers could return to Mexico for two weeks if they wished and still keep their jobs. "After three years, you can get two weeks of vacation and two weeks of leave of absence," the manager explained. That same plant also offered workers flexible scheduling so that they could take classes in English or other subjects.

On the other hand, one plant limits to three the number of times an individual can be rehired. Another plant limits rehires by requiring that employees wait for six months to pass since they were last employed. As a result, through a combination of industry and worker needs, the Hispanic workers are now remaining on the job, despite earlier documentation (e.g., Griffith 1993) of their high turnover rate. One personnel manager explained that this stabilization had occurred mainly in the last eighteen months, during which time annual turnover dropped from 160 percent to 50 percent (or 4 percent monthly). "I have Hispanic employees who have an average one-and-a-half to two years' seniority. Two years ago, this was less than a year. That deal of going back and forth [to Mexico] is not necessarily true," he pointed out. He also noted that in parts of Hall County there are increasing numbers of Hispanics purchasing houses. A contingent of Mexican workers continues to circulate, but according to one plant manager, fully 80 percent of the workers are stable. He characterizes the remaining 20 percent as "temps," because they usually work for only five or six months. A lot of people apparently planned to stay for only a short period, but the need to save money causes them to stay. An increasing number of Hispanic workers are finding that their savings go toward maintaining their lifestyles in the United States rather than returning to Mexico. In any event, both the circulating and the more stable Mexican workers are having lasting effects on the region. Not only is the social composition of the plants' employee population changing, but so are the kinds of music, cultural life, and businesses one finds in the area.

POPULATION CHANGE IN NORTH GEORGIA

The people I interviewed for this study were not the first Mexicans to come to North Georgia. The earliest Mexican workers in the poultry factories arrived in the 1970s, but there were no significant changes in the social composition of the population until the mid-1980s, the height of the economic crisis in Mexico. Census figures for that period indicate dramatic increases in the Hispanic population of towns where processing plants were located. For example, Gainesville had only 110 Hispanic residents (43 of whom were of Mexican origin) in 1980, when the total population was 15,280. But by 1990 there were 1,130 people of Mexican origin out of 4,558 Hispanics in a total population of 17,885. Local sources (e.g., poultry industry officials, the Chamber of Commerce, a Spanish-language newspaper), however, speculate that the overall Spanish-speaking population of Hall County, where Gainesville is located, is more likely between 12,000 and 30,000, indicating that the population may number approximately 2.6 to 6.6 times the official census count for the county.

Although some of these Hispanics came to Georgia via California, many now come directly from Latin America, especially Mexico. For example, the city of Gainesville school system is ranked twelfth in the state in terms of the number of students for whom English is a second language (Schrenko 1996). The overwhelming majority of these students (1,481 out of 1,635 children) are Spanish speakers. Processing workers enrolled in an ESL program indicated on intake forms that they were from Mexico. Supervisors, managers, nurses, and employment coordinators in many plants must be able to speak Spanish as a condition of their employment. Job advertisements are placed in both English and Spanish. At one plant, the personnel manager was Hispanic; he had begun working on the production line. The number of Hispanic immigrants working in the processing plants varies in the official statistics from 20 percent to 79 percent, although anecdotal information suggests that the actual numbers might be higher.

According to the restaurant owner, there were perhaps thirty Hispanic people working at the plant in Gainesville, where he got his start in 1985. But as another worker added, "When I came to Gainesville, I couldn't see a Mexican on the street. But now when you go, all you see are Mexicans." A plant manager explained, "At the beginning, we had only white folks. Then blacks. Then Vietnamese people. They are [mostly] gone now. They realized they can do something else and now we have Hispanics." One supervisor put the matter bluntly: "If there weren't Hispanic workers, nobody in America would be eating chicken."

INDUSTRIAL GROWTH AND WAGE STAGNATION

The arrival of Mexican workers in the poultry plants also has much to do with trends in production and wages. The U.S. broiler industry as a whole is the leading producer of chickens worldwide and is estimated to have produced 15,588,000 metric tons of ready-to-cook products in 1999, according to the Foreign Agricultural Service (FAS) of the U.S. Department of Agriculture (USDA). Exports of broiler meat, the average store-bought chicken, grew from approximately $200 million in 1985 to $1.9 billion in 1997, according to FAS. This process of globalization has been an important part of the North Georgia economy since the 1970s, when Gainesville first became known as "The Poultry Capital of the World." While its ranking has slipped, processing plants continue to have trade connections around the world. For example, companies in North Georgia earn 25 to 40 cents per pound on chicken feet (known as "paws" in the industry), which are sold in Asia. In addition to export growth, a drive down any strip mall in this country reveals the pervasiveness of chicken products in the American diet. U.S. broiler consumption per capita exceeded that of beef in 1992, and the country's broiler production exceeded that of beef in 1994. Per capita consumption is expected to increase twenty pounds between 1996 and 2005.

In order to meet rising demand, the industry increased production mainly by hiring more workers, because in this industry labor is cheaper than capital improvements. As a result, despite innovations in technology, production workers still perform much of the work on the disassembly lines. Depending on the portion of the line on which they work, they may stand alongside conveyor belts that shuttle slaughtered birds past them at rates between 90 and 180 chickens per minute (Horwitz 1994). "Everything is timed," explained a plant manager, from the number of birds hung in the hanging room per minute to the time it takes for the disassembled birds to reach the USDA inspectors. USDA policy has been to allow line speeds to increase to the fastest possible rate, with little regard for how workers can keep pace.

Workers at the poultry plants are, in effect, servants of the American consumers, whose rising incomes have transformed them into what one plant manager calls "Little Louis XIVs." Consumers gladly pay other people to do jobs—such as food preparation—that they consider beneath their dignity. At the same time, innovations in chicken genetics have made it possible to raise birds cheaper and faster to cater to consumers' increasing wariness about red meat. Consumers elsewhere in the world are increasingly echoing American consumers' preferences: 65 percent of employment growth in the industry is due to export growth between 1985 and 1996 (Department of Agriculture 1999).[2] In 1999 there were 219,400 poultry production line workers in the United States; it was one of the fastest growing jobs in the country in the early 1990s (Bureau of Labor Statistics 1996a, 1996b; Horwitz 1994).

The relative cheapness of labor in the poultry industry is largely a factor of the concentration of the industry in right-to-work states—those states that do not allow unions to demand union membership as a condition of employment. Wages are notoriously low in such states, and since 1972 the real wage in the industry has declined 10 percent.[3] In 1972 the poultry-processing and -slaughtering hourly wage was $5.75 in constant dollars. Today, although the national average hourly wage for poultry workers is about $8.42 (i.e., more than $3 above the minimum wage), the real value of the wage is approximately $5.25, fifty cents less than twenty-five years ago. The wage is the lowest in the entire food industry and one of the lowest in manufacturing (Hetrick 1994). Southern wages for poultry workers are typically lower than the national rate, averaging about $6.50 per hour (National Interfaith Committee for Worker Justice 1997). One of the consequences of the reliance on a low-wage labor force is that workers are getting less of a share of the value generated during their working day. The rate of value-added per hour of paid labor has increased dramatically in the past thirty years, whereas real wages have declined overall, and the real cost of chicken has dropped.[4]

Because of the stagnation of the poultry-processing wage, wage differentials within the United States also have a role in the transformation of the poultry industry. For this reason, plant managers told of workers native to the region seeking out "better jobs," forcing the industry to find new employees. One manager explained that "One of the big problems we have today is ten or fifteen years ago, we didn't have to compete. Now all of a sudden you get Duckhead [another company]. Now that all of the towns are becoming suburbs, we have to compete with other industries to get people to come work here." Somewhat isolated from larger cities, his plant's starting pay rate was twenty-five cents higher than at plants located closer to cities. Yet this same manager admitted that he currently has more job applicants than jobs available. Another manager said that new jobs in his county were drawing workers away from the plants. As native workers seek out better jobs, immigrant laborers more than make up the difference.

In order to replenish and increase their pool of workers, plant managers try to recruit new employees through state agencies and immigrant networks, as Griffith (1993) has shown. One of the workers I interviewed had arrived in Gainesville from Texas due to a state employment agency referral. I was told that this recruitment strategy no longer involves paying employees for bringing new workers to the plants. In the past, as I was told by the Mexican immigrant who became a restaurant owner, "The [poultry plant] owner was asking us for more Hispanic people. He would pay $50 for each Hispanic worker we brought to [the company]. From there, I called my cousin. He called his cousin, his brother-in-law. He gave money to one of my friends to pay for twelve people to come from Houston." Although no longer paid for such referrals, workers still routinely recruit family members, since they recognize the economic benefits of coming to work in the plants.

ONE OUTCOME OF ECONOMIC CRISIS

Mexico's current economic problems stem, at least in part, from the 1982 debt crisis. Mexicans began migrating to North Georgia during that crisis and continued to do so during the dislocations provoked by the devaluation of the *peso* in 1994, a move that caused inflation rates to increase precipitously (Economist Intelligence Unit 1997:8). In fact, twelve of the twenty-two immigrants I interviewed had arrived since the 1994 devaluation crisis. One woman told me, "They tell me the situation is the same as before I left. The salaries are minimal. Things [prices] rise every month." She explained that she wanted a better life for herself and her family, and that a relative had helped her plan her migration. She, in turn, has helped other relatives; indeed, she currently shares an apartment with six people, all of whom work at the same plant.

Other workers explained that their migration was determined by the lack of adequate employment opportunities in Mexico, where working-class people find it exceedingly difficult to support a family. One man told me, "In Mexico they make like 150 *pesos* a week. That's like $20 a week. People that know how to work in construction and that know how to build houses make a little more. They make about $250 *pesos* a week. But to eat meat in Mexico on Sunday, you have to save money and buy nothing else but beans and soup. It's expensive. To buy clothes for one person, pants cost 100 *pesos*. With one person with children and a wife, it's difficult." Another worker said that she ate meat in Mexico only once every eight days, but in the United States she is able to eat meat every day. She told me that she was always looking for "something better," a quest that first took her to Oregon, then to San Francisco, and finally to North Georgia, where she works on the deboning line of a poultry-processing plant, probably the most common job for women in this industry.

When asked what the economic crisis has meant to him, one immigrant said, "For me, it means never having everything you want. It means if you have a job, you will never be able to get the things to live comfortably. In Mexico, there is no way to have a new house or a new car. There is no way, unless you hit the lottery." This worker said that he had a degree in industrial engineering. Another worker I interviewed had been out of work in Mexico for some time. At a restaurant in Gainesville, he asked me whether I knew how he could acquire working papers, as he wanted to get a job in one of the poultry plants. Showing me a photo of his six children, he said, "I am here because they don't have anything to eat."

The immigrants have few employment options in the United States. Work in the poultry industry is one of the few jobs open to new arrivals.[5] One man who had been in Gainesville for twenty-five years said, "When I came over here, I didn't want to hang chicken because nobody wants to do that. But I was glad to have a job." Poultry-processing jobs do not, however, offer people much long-term satisfaction. One young woman complained that she does not like the United States simply because all there is for her is either work or the apartment, where she watches Spanish-language television. She was simply bored. Another worker agreed, saying, "There are a lot of people that go to a chicken plant, but after a while they get fed up and they look for other work. I really get bored because sometimes I don't have anything to do." Married to a U.S. citizen, this worker was studying for his General Education Diploma so that he could find work outside the plants.

CONCLUSION

It is difficult to observe changes in the immigrant populations in Georgia because Mexican and other Spanish-speaking immigrants often live in out-of-the-way places and are easily overlooked. Moreover, many people continue to migrate back and forth across the border. Nonetheless, the example of immigrant workers in Georgia demonstrates that the immigrant presence is both a growing and an increasingly stable one. The current situation is one that the migrants themselves have chosen and are relatively happy with, given their very limited options.

NOTES

Thanks to Andrew Herod, Kavita Pandit, Jim Wheeler, Gillian Hart, and Allan Pred for comments and assistance.

1. I call this district a Mexican enclave because most of the people interviewed for this study are Mexican, although there are certainly other Latin Americans living in North Georgia and working in the poultry industry in that area.

2. For data on employment trends in the poultry industry, see Hetrick (1994), Katz (1996), and Horwitz (1994).

3. In 1994, 84 percent of the broiler chickens raised in the United States were raised in the southern states (Bureau of Labor Statistics 1996b). Eleven of these states, including Georgia, are right-to-work states. The real wage is the actual wage adjusted for consumer price inflation. It indicates the purchasing power of a particular wage—i.e., what it can buy, given prices in a particular year. The real cost of chicken is the average cost of chicken adjusted for inflation. The dollar value is set to 1983–84 rates.

4. The value-added rate compares the value created by employees in one hour with the hourly wage they receive. I calculated this rate by subtracting from the Bureau of Labor Statistics index of output per employee hour among production workers in the poultry industry (Bureau of Labor Statistics 1996b) their national hourly wage in real dollars. This figure provides a rough estimate of the value created for the industry in one hour per employee. I then divided this number by the national average wage. This index shows how much more value is created for the industry versus how much employees earn on average in one hour. A rate of 10 means that the industry makes ten times the hourly wage per employee hour (Bureau of Labor Statistics 1996a).

5. Hard data are not available, but men in the processing plants appeared to work mainly in packaging, in the hanging rooms, and in the blast freezers.

REFERENCES

Bureau of Labor Statistics. 1996a. *National Employment, Hours and Earnings.* http://stats.bls.gov/top20.html (last accessed on June 10, 2000).

———. 1996b. *Poultry Dressing and Processing Plants (SIC 2015), All Years, Industry Productivity Index.* http://stats.bls.gov/iprhome.htm (last accessed on June 10, 2000).

Economist Intelligence Unit. 1997. *Country Report: Mexico First Quarter 1997.* London: Economist Intelligence Unit.

Firestone, D. 1999. Many See Their Future in Country with a Past. *New York Times,* April 8, A9.

Griffith, D. 1993. *Jones's Minimal: Low-wage Labor in the United States.* Albany: State University of New York Press.

Hetrick, R. 1994. Why Did Employment Expand in Poultry Processing Plants? *Monthly Labor Review* 117(6):31–34.

Horwitz, T. 1994. Nine to Nowhere. *Wall Street Journal,* December 1, B6.

Katz, J. 1996. The Chicken Trail: How Migrants Put Food on America's Table. *Los Angeles Times,* November 10–12, A15–20.

National Interfaith Committee for Worker Justice. 1997. *Poultry Facts.* Gainesville, Ga.: National Interfaith Committee for Worker Justice.

Schrenko, L. 1996. *The Status of Students of Limited English Proficiency in Georgia Public Schools.* Atlanta: Georgia Department of Education, Office of Instructional Services.

Stull, D., M. Broadway, and D. Griffith, eds. 1995. *Any Way You Cut It: Meat Processing and Small Town America.* Lawrence: University of Kansas Press.

U.S. Department of Agriculture, Foreign Agricultural Service. 1999. *All about Broiler Meat Exports.* http://www.fas.usda.gov (last accessed on June 10, 2000).

Walker, J. 1989. Segmentation Processes in Immigrant Incorporation: A Micro Analysis. Ph.D. diss., University of Utah.

Hospitality and Hostility:
Latin Immigrants in Southern Georgia

John D. Studstill and Laura Nieto-Studstill

The coastal plain of Georgia covers the southern half of the state. It is part of the ecological zone formed when an ancient ocean retreated across what is now a belt of flat, sandy land extending all the way from eastern Virginia to eastern Texas. This agricultural zone in Georgia is a land of small farms, piney woods, and wire grass. The geological characteristics of the area have resulted in a developmental path that distinguishes southern from northern Georgia; the latter is dominated by the urban colossus of Atlanta in the foothills of the Piedmont zone (Barlett 1993:23; Weatherington 1994:xxiii). Southern Georgia, like much of the South, was not really affected by the foreign immigration that transformed the rest of the United States in the first half of the twentieth century. It remained a predominantly agrarian area, but one dominated by small farmers and diversified crops rather than by the monocrop plantation economy of the Piedmont and the *Gone with the Wind* legend. Several recent studies have begun to fill in the complex history and sociology of this inadequately researched region of yeoman farmers (Malone 1981; Weatherington 1994), even as a new wave of immigration has begun to affect the area.

The sudden influx of Mexicans and other Latins has come as a shock to many in the area, although the native-born population appears to have been very hospitable to the newcomers, a surprising situation given the historically tense relations between white and black residents of South Georgia.[1] Significant sociocultural changes have also come to the region as a result of the growth of light industry, the consolidation of farms into moderate-sized agribusinesses, and the development of enormous forest holdings by paper and related companies. Migrant farmworkers from Latin America have arrived, and many former migrants have settled and found a more permanent niche in the area. The big out-migration of rural sharecroppers, both Euro and Afro, that began in the 1930s has thus been reversed. Now many small towns are slowly growing again, as the more dynamic counties draw local farm labor to small industries (Stack 1996). Although there are some Asians among the new migrants, most of the newcomers are Mexicans who have left the fields for the towns. Thus is written a new chapter in what Randy Ilg describes as "The Changing Face of Farm Employment" (1995) and in what Barbara Smith calls "The Postmodern South" (1998).

TRUE MIGRANTS AND THE SETTLED-OUT

Research for this study of Latins in rural Georgia began in 1996 and concentrates on Middle and South Georgia mainly because little research on the new immigrants has been done in that region. Despite its industrial underdevelopment, South Georgia has long been an important economic zone, producing peaches, peanuts, pigs, pecans, chickens, cattle, cotton, soybeans, tobacco, and watermelons, as well as the famed Vidalia onions, Moultrie tomatoes, and Tifton pickles. Our first impulse was to study migrant farmworkers, but our interest soon shifted to former migrants (those who have "settled out"), a group that has not been as frequently studied as the migrants themselves. The settled-out do not, however, constitute a homogeneous group. Most of them have left farmwork only recently, although others have never done farmwork at all. Some have moved from the Southwest to new industries in South Georgia; others, often with a military background, have come to the area to retire with their southern spouses. The true migrant farmworkers may or may not be citizens; they may have their home bases for the winter months in Georgia, Florida, or Mexico, and may be either legal or undocumented. Finally, there are those who return to the migrant stream if their new jobs do not work out.

To our knowledge, there are no precise statistics on these different categories, but it appears that the number of the settled-out now equals the number of seasonal migrants in the two counties we studied. A third category of legal, temporary guest workers (those with H-2A visas) is also being created in some locales. Temporary workers have long been used in some other states, but Georgia farmers are just beginning to experiment with the program due to pressures from the Immigration and Naturalization Service to reduce the number of undocumented workers. The actual number of settled-out Latins in Georgia is probably about double the official census count.

THE TWO COUNTIES

In this essay, we address four main questions: How many new Latins are there? What are they doing? How are they adjusting? How have they been received by the long-term residents? These issues were studied in Fruit County, in the peach-growing zone just south of Macon, and Tobacco County, farther south. Both counties (their names are pseudonyms) have economies based on agriculture, but they are more open to economic innovation than most areas of rural Georgia. Our research, which is based on participant observation and in-depth interviews with individuals identified through personal contacts, should be considered exploratory. Our goal is to describe how a sociocultural system or subsystem works.

According to published population statistics, each of these two counties has grown by about 15 percent between 1990 and 1997, although over 50 percent of the growth has been the result of in-migration rather than natural increase. About 25 percent of the new population is composed of Spanish-speakers, and the Latin minority has doubled in the space of a decade (Boatright and Bachtel 1998:146–47). Tobacco County is large in area but moderate in population density relative to the Georgia average. It is located near no urban center, but it has been attracting a certain amount of light industry since the 1960s on the initiative of several local entrepreneurs. Before that time, it had achieved only very modest prosperity based mainly on tobacco and peanuts. Now, however, it boasts a Wal-Mart distribution center, a chicken-processing plant, a small-engine manufacturer, and several mobile home assembly plants. One local entrepreneur has become a multi-millionaire by manufacturing components for the mobile home plants, all dependent on ex-migrants for much of their labor force. On the farms, both permanent and seasonal jobs are provided by tobacco cultivation, truck farming, pine straw bailing, and the raising of chickens. The local large farmers who employ migrant labor are often ambitious young men who rent acreage from others, a risky and unstable practice that is even more uncertain than the agribusinesses of the large peach growers in Fruit County. The soil in Tobacco County is sandy and less fertile than that of the old cotton belt of Middle Georgia. As a result, it never developed a plantation economy, a historical fact reflected in its small number of U.S.-Afros relative to Fruit County, which is on the edge of the old cotton plantation belt. Tobacco County is about 25 percent U.S.-Afro, the same as Georgia as a whole; Fruit County, by contrast, is nearly 50 percent Afro. Despite its prosperous large farmers, Fruit county had a family poverty rate of 25.2 percent in 1993, slightly higher than Tobacco County, which had a rate of 23.1 percent. The Georgia rate overall was itself a scandalous 17 percent (Boatright and Bachtel 1998:44–45).

Fruit County has several large peach and pecan growers who qualify as farming elites. In fact, the Euro population of Fruit County as a whole forms a virtual ethnic upper class and represents 48 percent of the total population, of whom only 7 percent are classified as poor. Tobacco County, by comparison, is 70 percent Euro, of whom 16 percent are poor (Boatright and Bachtel 1998:44–45). Since it is located near Macon, Fruit County includes a large number of people who commute to jobs in the city. It has also enjoyed the prosperity provided by light manufacturing plants and by a large military base. Fruit County's area is only one-fourth that of Tobacco County, but its total population is almost three-fourths that of its more southerly neighbor (24,000, compared to 34,000). Both of these counties are decidedly rural in character, but the majority of the people in each nonetheless work in the several small towns that dot the countryside. Tobacco County counts only 5.3 percent of its population as farmers, and Fruit County even fewer (1.3 percent). About 60 percent in each county live outside the urban areas but work in town (Boatright and Bachtel 1998:128–29).

THE NEWCOMERS

The settled-out Latins in the two counties are almost all of Mexican origin. The seasonal migrant workers are also mainly Mexican, although some Guatemalans (who speak only Mayan dialects, not Spanish) and other Central Americans have begun appearing. The ethnicity of the eastern stream of migrant farmworkers began to shift from Afro to Latin as early as the 1960s. Then in the 1980s an expanding wage-labor

economy in the South led to the steady filtering out of migrant farmworkers, despite the nationwide recession and the increasing disparity
between rich and poor.

U.S. census data typically undercount Latins but still provide a
baseline for estimating populations in Georgia. For example, the 1996
County Guide lists 899 Spanish speakers in Tobacco County (2.7 percent of the total population). Fruit County had 553 Latins (2.4 percent
of the total) (Boatright and Bachtel 1998:144–47). These figures are
almost certainly too low, for in Tobacco County in December 1998
(before the influx of migrant children that occurs in the spring and summer) there were nearly 400 Latin children enrolled in public schools, 5
percent of the total enrollment (*Statistical Summary* 1998:10). If 5 percent of the adult population is also Latin, there would be at least 2,000
Latins in the county. The estimated Latin population of the county is
therefore roughly double the official count, a situation that also obtains
in metropolitan Atlanta, as reported by the Georgia State University
Center for Applied Research in Anthropology (Dameron and Murphy
1997:50). Burns (1997:1-B) estimates that the Latin population of Fruit
County is about 5 percent, likewise double the official estimate of 2.4
percent. This figure may double again—or even triple—during the peak
harvest season. There are fewer seasonal migrants in Tobacco County
than in Fruit County, but even there the peak total of Latins is probably near 10 percent of the total population.

Census data for Tobacco County indicate that 70.8 percent of the
population is white, 28.4 percent is black, and 2.7 percent is Latin (with
0.7 classified as "other"). Beyond the problem of outmoded color terms,
one must note how these numbers mix false racial terms with ethnic
categories. Some Latins are in fact counted twice, once as "Hispanics"
and once as "Hispanic Blacks" (Boatright and Bachtel 1998:144–47),
although it has been estimated that about 2.5 percent of those listed as
"Black" are actually Latin. Our own observations lead us to estimate
that the permanent population of Tobacco County is 70 percent Euro,
25 percent Afro, and 5 percent Latin. In Fruit County, the figures would
be 48 percent Euro, 48 percent Afro, and 4 percent Latin. The currently
minuscule "other" category seems to be growing, but at a relatively slow
rate; Indians (i.e., from India) and Chinese seem to be particularly well
represented in professional positions (e.g., health care).

PROCESSES OF SETTLING OUT: FRUIT COUNTY

On Interstate 75 south of Macon stands a 200-foot high peach monument (the "Big Peach"), a landmark that helped bring a large Mexican family, the Ochoas, from Michoacán to Fruit County. When the Mexicans came through Georgia in 1981 fleeing the big freeze in the Florida orange groves, the head of the family remembered the Big Peach from an earlier visit and turned off the highway when he saw it again. That family became the nucleus of a Latin community in Peachtown, the county seat, that has been in residence for nearly twenty years. Peachtown proclaims itself to be a place "Where Caring is a Way of Life," and the Ochoas have found it to be so.

Papa Ochoa was fifty years old in 1981. After many years as migrant workers in California and Florida, he and his younger brother had recently become U.S. citizens and had brought their families to Florida. They continued to work in the eastern migrant stream as far north as Michigan. Although they were crew leaders and had managed to purchase homes near the orange groves, they still struggled to make ends meet. Their relocation to Fruit County proved to be a happy one. They impressed Grower Tom so much that he urged them to come back the next year with a bigger crew. He told them that their group of twelve did more work that first year than thirty local workers. Now that Papa Ochoa is retired, one of his sons, who is thirty-three years old and college educated, has taken over the role of permanent foreman and labor recruiter for Big Peach Farms. Other growers in the peach zone have followed a similar pattern, one even to the point of hiring other members of the Ochoa clan to do similar foreman and recruiting work.

The Ochoas and several other families have therefore developed a very positive, long-term relationship with the growers, and a whole new generation of workers has come to pick peaches and ended up putting down roots and getting permanent jobs. The younger Ochoa says that 10 to 20 of his approximately 200 workers tend to settle out in Fruit County each year, and this number is probably multiplied by a factor of ten if all the seasonal migrants hired by other growers in the county are factored in. At Big Peach Farms, the younger Ochoa is becoming a specialist in H-2A recruitment. Since the 1998 season, he has been recruiting workers in Michoacán, his home region. He signs contracts, helps workers get legal permits, supervises their transportation by commercial bus, and houses them in Big Peach Farms' own houses and trailers. He also organizes visits from the Mexican consul in Atlanta and arranges for recreation, hospital visits, and attendance at Sunday church services during the period of the workers' stay, generally April to August.

Lest this story sound overly idyllic, it should be noted that not everyone likes the H-2A program, mainly because they believe it takes away jobs, not only from undocumented workers but also from U.S. citizen migrants. In any case, these jobs are highly desired by many rural Mexicans. The younger Ochoa estimates that his Mexican workers earn between $7,000 and $11,000 for a season, although the wage varies due to a piece-rate system that involves the bucket-by-bucket monitoring of the picking by a sophisticated electronic device.

The five big growers in Fruit County produce approximately 90 percent of Georgia's commercial peaches, but this industry is in decline and is even threatened with extinction because the center of peach cultivation in the United States has moved to the San Joaquin Valley of California due to the fact that the California farmers grow in greater volume and can market their produce at lower cost and because competition from foreign growers has intensified. Those five growers, in fact, are all that remain of the eighty who farmed in the county just twenty years ago. One of the growers had to reduce peach acreage by one-third in 1998, putting in pecan trees instead. Production, he says, has been reduced by 50 percent in just six years. Such a trend could have a severe impact on the Ochoas and others who depend on peaches for their livelihood. If the peach growers turn to pecans, demand for migrant labor would dry up. The younger Ochoa, in fact, does not expect his own two sons to go into peaches, and he has enrolled them in the best private Catholic school in the area to make sure that they have other options when the time comes.

PROCESSES OF SETTLING OUT: TOBACCO COUNTY

Unlike Fruit County, Tobacco County produces no single dominant commodity, although several big farmers have hired many Mexican migrants in recent years to harvest tobacco, cucumbers for pickling, and tomatoes. Upon settling out, some of these migrants have found permanent work on dairy, chicken, and hog farms and in road construction. The majority who have permanent work, however, are employed at the several mobile home plants and the large chicken-processing plant.

The situation of the Latins in Tobacco County is illustrated by a story related by Miss Bea, who owns a small mobile-home rental park in one of the small towns in the county. The park has only ten units, with a total housing capability of approximately fifty adults and children. According to Miss Bea:

> The first Mexicans came to my park in Farmtown about 1984, a few years before my husband died. They paid their rent better than the blacks and poor whites I'd been renting to. I liked them and started carrying one or two Mexican children with me to the Baptist church. Now sometimes I take ten or twelve kids with me on Sunday. Sometimes I think they go mainly for the snacks. The parents are often working or resting on Sundays and they don't speak much English.
>
> They eat mostly Mexican food—like to cook out on grills. They have the biggest birthday parties I've ever seen, even if they don't have much money. They like to hang up a big sack full of candy inside. One guy has even opened up a little store uptown with tortillas, videos, and Mexican CDs. And some of their customs are even rubbing off on us now—refried beans, for example. The corn tortillas make good dumplings.
>
> The last three years I have had one white couple and several mixed couples—white women, Mexican men. I don't know if they are married or not. Most whites aren't renting these cheap trailers any more. There's this one group of apartments, Smith's, he's got all three races in there. There's a trailer park up in Oak Branch, but he only rents to blacks. Most of my occupants have steady jobs at the local plants, but I get some migrants too. One trailer had seven men for a few months last summer. They drank a lot, filled up a whole trash can with beer bottles in one night. At first I had a lot of single migrants, then gradually they went and got their wives or married locals. One wife I remember didn't speak any English and went back home after a year. One time I found a woman cooking outside on a fire. Her gas had run out, and she didn't know how to tell me. There's one couple who both have

jobs at the new lawn mower factory in Centerville. Most work at
Fleetwood or Golden Poultry or on farms. Several of the men
married local girls and moved out. Paco still lives with Betty—she
keeps her hair blond, like most of the others. I think the Mexicans
prefer blonds!

The preacher in Centerville has a mission there now, a pretty
big congregation. He stayed with me for a short time before he
moved to Centerville. Then I had two Spanish-speaking girls; one
was from Puerto Rico and one from Atlanta. They did missionary
work for several years. One of them married a Mexican and now
gives Spanish language courses at the college. I remember Maria;
she used to pray for fifteen minutes in her car before she cranked
up every morning—a real devoted Christian. I have some families
that have been with me for ten years. Paco and Betty have been
with me for six years. They say that the Mexicans at the mobile-
home plants will do twice as much work as the whites. I've had a
few blacks from time to time in my trailers, but blacks don't
accept the Mexicans as much as the whites do. Some of the whites
weren't too friendly at first, but they have changed. There was one
woman at my church that didn't like me bringing the Mexican
children to Sunday school. She said, "Why don't they go to their
own church?" But later I saw her helping out with the children,
and one Sunday I remember seeing one of the little boys sitting
with her—he went to sleep on her lap.

There were seven children who learned to swim in my pool in
the back yard—kept begging to come up and swim. The little boys
learned by themselves, and then they helped the little girls. We
don't have any blacks or Mexican adults in our church. We do
have this Jesus tape, provided by the Baptist church. We gave one
to anyone who did not attend church. We now have it in Spanish.
A wealthy man in Alabama gave one to every family in Alabama.
Many don't understand our English services very well. Our church
has started picking up the Mexican kids in the church van. There
are about fourteen children who go to our church. Some parents
come on special occasions. These families need love and understanding. The farmers cannot harvest the crops without these
special people.

This interview reveals a great deal about how rapid, albeit superficial, the integration of many new immigrants has been. By contrast, just down the street from Miss Bea lives a Mexican woman from a well-to-do family from Monterrey. She has two children, has been working in the migrant education program for several years, and is married to a local man she met while he was ferrying migrant workers from Mexico. In her case a more complete integration is occurring, and with a higher rate of intermarriage Latins could gradually merge with the Euro population. But that outcome seems unlikely in the near future, although this educator emphasized how well she (and her visiting relatives) have been received by the long-time residents of Farmtown.

Another perspective is provided by the priest in Centerville, which has the only Catholic church in the county. Originally from Ireland, he has recently been posted for a second time as a missionary to South Georgia after a stint of several years in Ecuador. Father Sean says he has a total of about 200 congregants at his two English masses and 220 on average at the one Spanish mass. He had no Mexican parishioners until about 1980. As for other minorities, he has a grand total of 3 Afros in his congregation. He has performed only one marriage between a Mexican man and a U.S.-Euro woman, but he knows of a number of unmarried mixed couples living together. They tend to come to his attention after automobile accidents and at baptisms of their children.

According to another church worker, there is little police harassment of Latins, but the one situation that might qualify on this count is the setting up of roadblocks on weekends near some of the mobile-home parks to trap undocumented aliens and those without valid driver's licenses and auto insurance.

LATIN INTEGRATION AND ACCEPTANCE BY THE NATIVE-BORN

The younger Ochoa has observed the rapid acceptance of Mexicans in Fruit County. He laughs when he describes how in 1983 his cousin was unable to get credit to buy a car from a local dealer. "He had to go to Orlando to get one. Now the salesmen say, 'Oh, just go ahead and try it for a few days. You can pay me later.'" Ochoa and other foremen get numerous calls from local businesses asking if they have some Mexi-

can workers they can send over to work at the lumberyard or in landscaping in Macon. In short, the middlemen and the workers are locally
recognized and popular—particularly the middlemen, who have also
become middle class. Although there is longstanding evidence of poor
living conditions for many migrant farmworkers, we found little evidence of extreme cruelty or exploitation in the two counties under study.
We heard of only one case of extreme violence in a county adjacent to
Tobacco County; a Mexican crew leader had allegedly been murdered
several years ago by farmworkers whom he had cheated. Nonetheless,
horror stories surface from time to time throughout the South (Chepesiuk 1992).

Some of the Euro and Afro working class may not have been as wel-
coming of the new immigrants as the Euro employers have been, although we have found little evidence of overt hostility. Since the Mexicans still account for only 5 percent of the population in a growing
economy, they are not yet perceived as a threat. The younger Ochoa
says that the Afros do not seem to mind seeing the Mexicans move in,
but he sometimes senses some jealousy at how close he and his father
have become to Grower Tom. He thinks that the problems between
Afros and Euros have a long history and will be hard to overcome; the
Mexicans, however, do not share this burden of the past. He also feels
that Latins in general think that Afros are less willing than the Latins
are to sweat and work hard at jobs paying minimum wage. Moreover,
he has not yet met "a single Latin who works for a black man."

Grower Tom says the changeover from Afro workers began in the
early 1970s, at which time he had 250 local hires during peak work
months. Now he has about 30 permanent Afros who work all year, although they work mostly with pecans. There was some fear of job loss
the first few years when he began to hire Jamaicans and Haitians, but
he thinks most locals had by then decided that they did not want to continue working as farm laborers. One local black leader came to Tom
expressing concern about unemployed blacks; Tom told him that he
would rather hire locals if he could, but that it was difficult to put together a crew of fifteen drawn from Peachtown residents, whereas the
growers needed at least 2,000 workers. Tom himself needed 100 workers at that time just in his packing house, although he had only 15 local applicants. After that conversation there had been no further protest, and if there were hard feelings, he is sure he would know about it.

Tom adds:

> I can call black leaders and find out what's going on. We elected
> the last mayor together. It's not like in the 1950s any more. They
> can make $10 an hour and start in a lot of nearby industries, with
> benefits, so they aren't interested in seasonal farm work any more.
> A few years ago we could still hire 20 to 30 high school kids in
> the packing house during summer vacation. Now I can hardly get
> 5 or 10. Five or six years ago they stopped the old system of
> ending the school year early so students could work in the packing
> houses. In the 1950s we might hire 50 to 70 students just in our
> packing house, and there were sixteen houses in Peachtown alone,
> twenty-five within a five-mile radius. All that has changed. No one
> around here wants to work in peaches any more.

It would appear that in neither county has competition for jobs created hostility between locals and newcomers, but this situation could
change in an economic downturn. The number of intermarriages between Mexicans and Euros, and the lower level of racism implied by
such unions, make U.S.-Afros understandably wary, if not angry—a
topic that needs more careful research in the Afro community itself.

The integration of the new Latins in both counties seems to have been
almost too easy and too good to be true. It is worth noting, however,
that in Fruit County at least, a concerted effort spearheaded by the big
growers was organized to head off problems. The growers talked to the
police chief, took crew leaders to meetings of the Kiwanis Club, worked
with parks and recreation officials to organize Sunday soccer matches,
checked up on tax lawyers to make sure that they did not abuse the
workers in a tax-refund scam, invited the younger Ochoa to speak at
the Methodist church, carefully explained their situation to other business leaders at the Chamber of Commerce, held a health fair each spring,
helped get a Spanish-speaking teller hired at the bank, encouraged local merchants to stock Mexican food, and worked with the Catholic
church to establish a mission for aiding migrants in need of food, legal
assistance, health care, and English lessons.

Tobacco County has no organized effort of this sort, and yet as Miss
Bea's story demonstrates, individual small-scale humanitarian efforts,
in combination with church missions and economic self-interest, have
eased the integration of the newcomers. The one area of concern and

potentially increased friction continues to be the existence of many un-documented workers. INS raids disrupt the economy and disgust almost everyone in one way or another. They create bad feelings toward the government on the part of growers and workers, toward the growers on the part of humanitarians who believe the undocumented workers are underpaid and exploited, and toward the undocumented workers themselves on the part of the less informed segments of the commu-nity. This potentially disruptive ill will has encouraged the growers to support the H-2A program.

HOSPITALITY AND HOSTILITY

Our research suggests that hospitality has largely outweighed hostility toward the new immigrants in rural Georgia. The hospitality probably stems from economic self-interest rather than from the traditional val-ues of the presumably gracious old South, and so the situation could change if economic conditions worsen. The three major ethnic groups still see themselves as distinctive entities. Neither social integration nor intermarriage has progressed to a point where the three groups could easily see their interests as converging in the event of an economic downturn. But in the meantime, the relative prosperity of the region has made it possible for the Latins to be given a perhaps surprisingly posi-tive welcome. The major blight on this situation is the continuing rate of poverty among Afros in both counties—over 40 percent in both counties (Boatright and Bachtel 1998:44–45); there is no reason to believe that the rate for the Latin newcomers is any lower. Moreover, the rate for the seasonal migrants is probably 100 percent. With pov-erty still so widespread in a growing economy, one must be seriously apprehensive about future hard times. In the meantime, however, the best conclusion we can reach about the new multiculturalism in South Georgia is expressed by an elderly farmer: "'Round here folks say the Mexicans are all right. They talk like they're real hardworkin' and say it looks like the big farmers can't hardly get along without 'em."

NOTE

1. For the rest of this essay we will use the terms Euro, Afro, and Latin, rather than such terms as white, black, Hispanic, Euro-American, and African

American, unless quoting someone else's more color-based and ethnocentric terminology. We have used these terms elsewhere (Studstill 1998a, 1998b) because they refer to cultural categories, rather than to presumed "color" differences. They are also specific to social conditions and intergroup relations in the United States and do not presume universal "racial" categories.

REFERENCES

Barlett, P. 1993. *American Dreams, Rural Realities: Family Farms in Crisis.* Chapel Hill: University of North Carolina Press.

Boatright, S., and D. Bachtel, eds. 1998. *The Georgia County Guide.* Athens: University of Georgia Center for Agribusiness and Economic Development.

Burns, J. 1997. Field of Dreams. *Macon Telegraph*, August 14, 1-B.

Chepesiuk, R. 1992. Peonage for Peach Pickers. *The Progressive*, December, 22–24.

Dameron, R., and A. Murphy. 1997. An International City Too Busy to Hate? Social and Cultural Change in Atlanta, 1970–1995. *Urban Anthropology* 26:43–69.

Ilg, R. 1995. The Changing Face of Farm Employment. *Monthly Labor Review*, April, 3–11.

Malone, A. 1981. Piney Woods Farmers of South Georgia, 1850–1900: Jeffersonian Yeomen in an Age of Expanding Commercialism. *Agricultural History* 60:51–84.

Smith, B. 1998. The Postmodern South: Racial Transformations and the Global Economy. In *Cultural Diversity in the U.S. South*, eds. C. Hill and P. Beaver, 164–78. Athens: University of Georgia Press.

Stack, C. 1996. *Call to Home: African Americans Reclaim the Rural South.* New York: Basic Books.

Statistical Summary of Enrollments. 1998. Douglas, Ga.: County Board of Education.

Studstill, J. 1998a. A Rose by Any Other Name: A Modest Yet Radical Proposal about "America." *Voices of Mexico* 45:61–65.

——. 1998b. On Race, Ethnicity and Baby's Bathwater. *Anthropology Newsletter* 39:16–17.

Weatherington, M. 1994. *The New South Comes to Wiregrass Georgia, 1860–1910.* Knoxville: University of Tennessee Press.

Another Day in the Diaspora: Changing Ethnic Landscapes in South Florida

David Griffith, Alex Stepick, Karen Richman,
Guillermo Grenier, Ed Kissam, Allan Burns,
and Jeronimo Camposeco

In the past half-century, and especially since the Cuban Revolution of 1959 and the Civil Rights movement of the 1960s, South Florida has been a principal destination for people from the Caribbean, Mexico, Central America, and South America. How new immigrants settle into South Florida's social landscape is influenced by a variety of factors, including the ways that immigrant-receiving governments interact with immigrants and minorities, economic opportunities, currents of racism and prejudice, and local developments in neighborhoods and schools (Griffith 1998; Levitt 1998; MacDonald and Zaharlick 1994; Portes 1997).

One way of teasing out the relative influences of state policy, labor markets, ethnicity, and neighborhood dynamics is through comparative analysis that is richer than it is representative—that is, by collecting data on households, neighborhoods, work histories, political activities, and ethnic consciousness from small groups of immigrants and minorities and considering these data in light of wider social processes. We attempt to do so in this essay, as we compare five groups in South Florida in terms of several variables that reflect their everyday experiences. The groups were selected specifically because they have been incorporated into the South Florida political economy in distinctive ways. They include one refugee group that the state has embraced (Cubans), two refugee groups that the state has neglected to embrace (Guatemalans and Haitians), one immigrant group with a significant and growing minority presence in the United States (Mexicans and Mexican-Americans), and one native minority group that continues to suffer in the labor market and vis-à-vis the state (African Americans).

We emphasize that our samples are by no means representative. We do not present these data so as to extrapolate our findings to African Americans, Cubans, Guatemalans, Haitians, Mexicans, or Mexican-Americans elsewhere in the United States. Instead, we hope to enrich the ethnography of one area within the country that is currently receiving large numbers of immigrants, most of whom move into jobs and neighborhoods already populated by native minorities and other immigrants. We compare these groups by household composition, household and neighborhood changes, economic behavior, political activity, and ethnic consciousness.

HOUSEHOLDS AND NEIGHBORHOODS

We targeted urban neighborhoods in the long, narrow metropolitan area that extends from Rivera Beach to Miami along Florida's east coast and rural neighborhoods in Indiantown and Immokalee, two inland farming communities. We specifically targeted multiethnic neighborhoods. (For detailed descriptions, see Burns 1993; Grenier and Stepick 1994; Griffith 1997; Griffith and Kissam 1995.) Except for about half of the Cubans, all the respondents lived in neighborhoods dominated by low rents and crowded housing. Most of the neighborhoods featured businesses common to poor sections, such as convenience stores, liquor stores, pawn shops, and check-cashing services, along with several closed-up businesses and abandoned buildings or houses, a church or two, and various public and private social services (e.g., free clinics, domestic violence shelters). A few of the neighborhoods had seen the recent emergence of immigrant-owned services and businesses that serve the general population, as well as businesses such as bookstores, heritage centers, or funeral homes that cater primarily to the immigrants.

We asked several questions about household composition, including employment statuses, demographic information on household members, and length of residence in the current dwelling. There were also follow-up questions about changes in the neighborhood and in the household, as well as about other households with which the respondents interacted on a regular basis.

The Cubans and African Americans have been in residence for the longest continuous period, and both of those groups are characterized by nuclear and extended family households. The more recently arrived Haitians and Guatemalans, by contrast, have households composed of several adults, usually lateral kin. They also have what we call *anchor households*, in which one nuclear family hosts (on a temporary basis) newly arrived lateral kin. Households among the newly arrived immigrants tend to change because of the influx of additional relatives, whereas change among the more established groups occurs because of common life-cycle developments (e.g., children leaving home, elderly parents moving in).

ECONOMIC BEHAVIOR

In addition to brief work histories and accounts of current employment, data were collected on social and ethnic compositions of work places, multiple sources of income, job change and search behaviors, and discrimination in the work place. We paid particular attention to the concentration of certain groups in certain industries.

The most obvious distinction, again contrasting African Americans and Cubans with the other three groups, is the extent to which the newer immigrants remain confined to largely unskilled positions. Most of the Mexicans and Mexican-Americans and nearly all the Guatemalans worked in agriculture and related occupations such as landscaping. The Haitians had found work at the low end of service occupations, such as nurse's aides in nursing homes. The African Americans and Cubans are dispersed across several occupations (including government service) and skill levels; they also seem to be relatively stable in their occupations.

POLITICAL BEHAVIOR

We broadly define political behavior to include activities such as applying for government assistance; participating in labor unions; joining neighborhood, ethnic, and church groups; and attending political rallies or protest meetings. These behaviors express membership in a community that attempts to increase its members' power and advantage relative to the state, suggesting forms of leadership and customary methods for achieving political goals. Two observations encouraged us to adopt this very broad definition: first, in most cases, participation in established and institutionalized political contexts such as labor unions and political parties was extremely low; second, our informants themselves implied that they exercised political power in informal ways beyond those traditional institutions.

The data suggest that Cubans are the most active in formal political institutions, since they join parties and unions and list local politicians among their leaders. African Americans also participate in formal political institutions but are more likely than the Cubans to exert power in the community through the church and other associations that are not technically political. The newcomers, particularly the Haitians and Mexicans, were apparently more interested in political developments in their homelands than in the United States, although they recognize the advantages of being aware of—and learning how to access—state support services. Many of the Guatemalans belonged to an ethnic association called Corn Maya, but on the whole they were far less politically active than any of the other groups.

ETHNICITY AND INTERETHNIC RELATIONS

We probed for information on ethnicity by asking several questions about respondents' own and other ethnic groups. After eliciting a free listing of ethnic groups, we asked their opinions about which of the named groups were more or less empowered and which were more or less economically advantaged. We then asked about their own interactions with other groups and encouraged them to evaluate their own group in terms of factors that distinguish them from other groups, particularly with regard to a work ethic.

In many ways, these responses were the most revealing of how the processes of immigrant adjustment and native response to immigration are worked out in South Florida. The specific responses discussed below tend to be widely shared *within* each group, even though the groups differ radically in their estimation of others' experiences and positions of power and economic opportunity.

African Americans

Most African Americans consider themselves politically empowered relative to other ethnic groups in South Florida, although they lament that this power has not translated into economic opportunity. In their free lists, they name up to twenty-three ethnic groups, with most of the distinctions based either on nationality (e.g., Colombian) or racial classifications (e.g., white, Arab, Hispanic). Of the groups they listed, they interacted most frequently with West Indians (especially African Caribbean people); they had the least contact with the Guatemalans, whom they also considered to be the least empowered and the least economically successful group.

The African Americans had somewhat negative self-images, characterizing their group as "uncooperative," "uncommunicative," and unwilling to work together effectively. They saw themselves as having poor work habits relative to other groups, and they believed that many members of their community think that the government owes them a living. These ideas were expressed even by those who had themselves been gainfully employed throughout their lives.

The interviews elicited only a handful of positive comments. One person said, "Other ethnic groups have less connections as to who to contact in case of problems." Two others said that African Americans "take pride in their work" and are "more educated than other groups." Perhaps the most positive statement, however, came from a woman who said, "We're hard-working, loving people. We care for each other. We're a very spiritual people, and we depend on God more than others."

Haitians

Haitians saw themselves as among the least economically successful groups, and perhaps because they assumed their lack of success to be a factor of prejudice against blacks in general, they did not agree with the African Americans' self-assessment as empowered. They listed Cubans, Jews, and whites in general as examples of groups that were truly empowered and economically successful, with Mexicans and non-Cuban Latinos joining their own community at the bottom of the political and economic heap. Nearly all Haitians believed that government agencies, employers, police, and other authorities discriminate heavily against them in South Florida.

The Haitians interact primarily with other West Indians, including those who speak English or Spanish rather than Creole. Indeed, the Haitians were very careful in their listing of ethnic groups to distinguish people from the many small islands of the Caribbean, rather than grouping them all in a single category. Few Haitians interacted with African Americans on a regular basis, although they shared the self-assessment of the latter as uncooperative and lacking in solidarity. The Haitians were apt to characterize each other in negative terms, using adjectives like "insolent" and "full of themselves." They claimed that they tended to form small, closed cliques rather than community-wide associations.

Guatemalans

In their free listing of ethnic groups in South Florida, the Guatemalans named fewer groups than the others and also tended to list Spanish-speaking groups from Latin America and the Caribbean, with whom they report the most frequent interactions. This tendency might reflect the fact that they and the Mexicans work together in the farm labor market. They considered the Puerto Ricans to be empowered because of their bilingual abilities, although in general they avoided responding to questions about either political or economic empowerment. They did not include Middle Easterners or Jews at all, although some recognized African Americans, whom they referred to as *Moyos*. While a few made distinctions among different indigenous populations (e.g., Jacaltec or Mam Mayan), most of them lumped all Guatemalans together. They liked to emphasize their Native American heritage, saying, for example, "Our history is different," or "Most of us are Indians. It is our weakness and our strength at the same time."

The Guatemalans saw themselves as dedicated to hard work, even though they usually got the worst jobs in South Florida. Nevertheless, it is important for them to work hard even at unattractive jobs because the situation in Guatemala is so bad that their families back home are absolutely dependent on them to send back money.

Mexicans and Mexican-Americans

The Mexicans' lists of ethnic groups were longer than those of the Guatemalans, but they likewise tended to include mostly Spanish-speaking groups. They made finer distinctions among the latter, however, identifying Tejanos (those from Texas), Puerto Ricans, Colombians, Salvadorans, and so forth. Like the Guatemalans, they spent their time primarily with other Mexicans and Spanish-speaking people.

Most of the Mexicans believed that whites (*bolillos*) had the most rights and the most power in the United States, but they did not attribute this situation to blatant ethnic discrimination. For example, they were apt to say that anyone with "papers" (legal documentation) had power, and that anyone who spoke English had access to political power and economic opportunity. Those who came directly from Mexico to Florida expressed some ambivalence about those who had come via Texas beginning in the 1950s. The Mexicans saw the latter as having the great advantages of both citizenship and English language ability and yet as having failed to build on these assets (Griffith 1997). The Mexican-Americans stayed in the farm labor market, gradually working their way into labor contracting, albeit without much success. The Mexicans saw the Mexican-Americans' failure to capitalize on their advantages as the reason that they were stuck in the rut of farm labor.

Cubans

Like Haitians, Cubans seemed particularly sensitive to ethnic differences among South Floridians, splitting rather than lumping together several different ethnic groups from Europe, the Middle East, South America, and the Caribbean. Within this varied ethnic landscape, they tend to be relatively restricted in their interactions, reporting that they spend most of their time with other Cubans or other Latinos. Only a few listed Anglos among their friends.

Over one-third of the Cubans listed themselves (and other Hispanics or Latinos) as the most powerful groups in the region; only one-quarter of them said that the Anglos were the most powerful. Jews and African Americans were also cited as having considerable political power. Jews, Anglos, and Cubans were seen as the most economically successful groups, while Haitians, African Americans, and non-Cuban Latinos were seen as the least successful.

The Cubans were especially positive about themselves as an ethnic group, particularly with regard to their work ethic. They described themselves as "upwardly mobile" and "hard-working," and they did not see themselves as being the objects of discrimination in South Florida. Many said that Cubans will persevere and never give up, even in the face of extreme hardship, and that they will continue to work happily and hard. While several acknowledged that Cubans received preferential treatment from the U.S. government because of the political connotations of their refugee status, they added that they have used these advantages to improve, rather than simply maintain, their economic and political positions.

CONCLUSIONS

Although the African Americans and Cubans we interviewed were similar to one another in several ways (e.g., household composition, distribution throughout the South Florida economy, use of government assistance), they evaluated themselves in very different ways. African Americans were overwhelmingly negative when characterizing their collective experience and work ethic, while Cubans were very positive. Cubans spoke of themselves as highly cooperative, while African Americans considered themselves to be uncommunicative and uncooperative.

Recent historical experiences may shed some light on these differences in perception. Cubans began fleeing their homeland in the wake of the 1959 revolution, settling with U.S. government assistance in several locations. Many of them, however, eventually made their way back to South Florida, especially the Miami area. "As early as 1972," according to Perez (1992:87–88), "there was increasing evidence that a 'trickle-back' . . . to Miami had begun. The concentration of Cubans in South Florida increased during the 1980s."

During the same period, African American neighborhoods in South Florida were affected by the desegregation policies of the time. African Americans were dispersed throughout South Florida's social landscape, as wealthier, more highly educated families moved away from traditional African American communities (Cecelski 1994; Dunn and Stepick 1992:50). Moreover, there was increasing immigration from the Caribbean, and these new black immigrants tended to settle in neighborhoods once dominated by African Americans (Griffith 1995). Relations between African Caribbeans and African Americans have not always been harmonious. Therefore, while the Cuban neighborhoods were consolidating, the black neighborhoods were fragmenting. The African American dispersal might have yielded results analogous to transnational migration—that is, the widening of networks in ways that assure access to new jobs, better opportunities for business, increased sharing of child-rearing duties, gift exchange, and consumption-pooling arrangements (such as several people contributing to buy a car)—but these results have not been much in evidence (Basch, Glick-Schiller, and Blanc 1995; Goldring 1990).

As for the other three groups, Haitians and Guatemalans reflect early phases of immigrant adjustment to South Florida, while the Mexicans and Mexican-Americans reflect an intermediate phase between the Haitians and Guatemalans on the one hand and the Cubans on the other. Early adjustment involves establishing households of several adults and devoting considerable energy to the business of simply being an immigrant: negotiating a limited range of employment opportunities while attempting to achieve a recognized legal status, arranging for remittances or the passage of relatives from home, helping to build an ethnic association, or devoting energies to the membership requirements of the enclave. During the initial phase of adjustment, it seems that political activity is nonexistent, oriented toward the homeland, or directed narrowly toward the issue of legal status. As such, it tends not to involve contesting conditions of work or asserting rights to education or government assistance. The Mexicans' assertion that power comes to anyone with papers drives home the point that being an immigrant permeates the identities of the foreign-born and colors their assessments of power and opportunity.

Later phases of adjustment involve elaborating households through the addition of more and more family members, particularly lineal kin. A more complex household may facilitate integration into the community, as children and elder family members require a fuller range of services than young adults living under dormitory-like conditions. It may also involve home ownership and a household's introduction to credit and other financial resources, further enmeshing families in South Florida society while creating stable households that offer new immigrants the opportunity to use the household as a base from which to seek new housing and employment. These households become particularly strategic locations for people who work in temporary jobs that require migration, most notably agriculture. Grey (1999) found this situation to be typical among Latino meatpacking workers in Iowa, and several developments in the international economy portend increasing tendencies among workers to combine temporary and seasonal work with self-employment. For example, subcontracting arrangements have long been the cornerstone of the garment industry, agriculture, and construction because of their ability to expand and reduce labor supplies with rapid shifts in markets or other parts of the production process. Such arrangements seem likely to assume even more importance as investors embrace a strategy of flexible accumulation. Future research will be needed to determine if these developments will result in more complex households among immigrant and minority groups.

NOTE

This article is based on data collected under the project titled "Immigrant Adjustment and Interethnic Relations in South Florida," funded by the National Science Foundation (DBS–9211620), along with a related project funded by the Howard Heinz Endowment. Many thanks to these agencies for their generous support, as well as to Maria Batik, John Brown, Sue Chafee, Anna Garcia, Ivory Hamilton, Laura Porro, and Yves Waterman for providing valuable research assistance.

REFERENCES

Basch, L., N. Glick-Schiller, and C. Blanc. 1995. *Nations Unbound: Transnational Projects, Postcolonial Predicaments, and Deterritorialized Nation-States*. Langhorne, Pa.: Gordon and Breach.

Burns, A. 1993. *Maya in Exile: Guatemalans in Florida*. Philadelphia: Temple University Press.

Cecelski, D. 1994. *Along Freedom Road: Hyde County and the Fight over Black Schools in the South*. Chapel Hill: University of North Carolina Press.

Dunn, M., and A. Stepick. 1994. Blacks in Miami. In *Miami Now: Immigration, Ethnicity, and Social Change*, ed. G. Grenier and A. Stepick, 25–49. Gainesville: University of Florida Press.

Goldring, L. 1990. *Development and Migration: A Comparative Analysis of Two Mexican Migrant Circuits*. Washington, D.C.: Commission for the Study of International Migration and Cooperative Development.

Grenier, G., and A. Stepick. 1994. Introduction. In *Miami Now: Immigration, Ethnicity, and Social Change*, ed. G. Grenier and A. Stepick, 1–14. Gainesville: University of Florida Press.

Grey, M. 1999. Immigrants, Migration, and Worker Turnover at the Hog Pride Pork Packing Plant. *Human Organization* 58:16–27.

Griffith, D. 1995. Names of Death: An Essay. *American Anthropologist* 97:453–56.

———. 1997. Lasting Firsts. *American Anthropologist* 99:23–29.

———. 1998. Experiencing Refugees: A Review Essay. *Reviews in Anthropology* 27:407–24.

Griffith, D., and E. Kissam. 1995. *Working Poor: Farmworkers in the United States*. Philadelphia: Temple University Press.

Levitt, P. 1998. Social Remittances: Migration-Driven, Local-Level Forms of Cultural Diffusion. *International Migration Review* 32:926–48.

MacDonald, J., and A. Zaharlick, eds. 1994. *Selected Papers on Refugee Issues.* Vol. 3. Arlington, Va.: Committee on Refugee Issues, General Anthropology Division, American Anthropological Association.

Perez, L. 1992. Cuban Miami. In *Miami Now: Immigration, Ethnicity, and Social Change*, ed. G. Grenier and A. Stepick, 50–75. Gainesville: University of Florida Press.

Portes, A. 1997. *Transnational Communities: Their Emergence and Significance in the Contemporary World System.* Baltimore: Department of Sociology, Johns Hopkins University.

Language and the Migrant Worker Experience in Rural North Carolina Communities

Jack G. Dale, Susan Andreatta, and Elizabeth Freeman

Agriculture is one of North Carolina's most important industries; in 1996 the state ranked eighth among the states for total farming income (Department of Commerce 1998). In addition, North Carolina ranks first among all states in the production of tobacco and third in the raising of poultry (Department of Agriculture 1998). The majority of agricultural workers are migrants who typically live in temporary housing. There are also agricultural laborers who are permanent local residents (North Carolina Farmworker Health Alliance 1996).

Migrant farmworkers arrive in the United States through both formal (labor contracts) and informal (transnational networks) means. Most labor arrangements involve a certain degree of mobility and seasonality. In order to provide for their personal needs, migrant workers must seek employment both inside and outside agriculture at various times of the year. When the local labor market becomes saturated, workers may have to relocate according to the seasonality of the crops, a survival strategy that can take them up and down the eastern seaboard, and sometimes beyond.

North Carolina serves as a useful case study for examining the changes in the labor force due to immigration. In the United States, North Carolina ranks fifth in total number of migrant farmworkers. More than 90 percent of the state's migrant farmworker population is of Hispanic origin, with the majority of workers coming from Mexico and

Central America. Local farmers now rely less on African American residents and more heavily on Hispanic immigrants (North Carolina Farmworker Health Alliance 1996). As a consequence, the Spanish-speaking population of the state has doubled in seven years, and although exact numbers are difficult to obtain, it is estimated that there are 150,000 Hispanics out of a total population of 7.4 million. Leaders in the community, however, suggest that there may be as many as 250,000 Hispanics (*National Agricultural Workers* 1997; "Compañía Manufacturera" 1998). The number of Latin American children enrolled in public schools has tripled since 1991 ("Hispanic Populace" 1998). By all accounts, the Hispanic population is in transition from a temporary migrant to a permanent resident status.

Agriculture is not necessarily the main source of income for migrant workers. Some move completely out of agriculture and into other labor sectors, while others rely on agriculture only for additional income. The movement away from agriculture can produce many new needs, such as the desire to attain some degree of English proficiency. Migrant workers view English as an important tool for socioeconomic advancement and for building community. This essay therefore examines how language proficiency relates to housing, employment, education, and health care as experienced by Hispanic migrant workers, particularly those who have decided to settle out of agriculture.

MIGRATION AND PATTERNS OF SETTLEMENT

The nature, direction, and end results of acculturation and related processes have all been variously interpreted. We understand acculturation to be defined by the social and cultural changes resulting from contact between groups, a process that occurs when two or more groups have firsthand and continuous contact with each other (Murphy 1989).

Assimilation theory has been subjected to intense criticism for decades and is currently in some disrepute (Alba and Nee 1997). "Fitting in" has been seen in the past as an all-or-nothing affair in which an embattled minority group has no choice but to accept the majority culture. The minority group may try to maintain its ethnic and cultural integrity, but it was thought that they would ultimately either assimilate or suffer the consequences (Barrera 1988). Resistance to assimilation leads to the characterization of the majority as a racist entity that will not allow the newcomers to integrate even though it proclaims the ideology of integration (Skerry 1993). Americans have historically been inclined to celebrate the history of immigration and the concept of the melting pot even while criticizing multiculturalism in all its forms (De Wind and Kasinitz 1997).

We argue, however, that assimilation and acculturation need not be unilinear, monolithic processes. It is possible that cultural traits are transmitted in both directions, not necessarily top-to-bottom, majority-to-minority. The narrow conception of acculturation as the wholesale substitution of one culture for another does not account for the influence of minority ethnic cultures on mainstream Euro-American society. For example, minority ethnic traits can be mixed with mainstream elements to create a hybrid cultural mix (Alba and Nee 1997). In effect, a minority uses or discards the traits it deems appropriate even in the absence of overt coercion (Monsivais 1995).

One of the most important tools at the disposal of newly arrived immigrants is language, and one of the most important survival strategies is the development of language proficiency. The migrant worker therefore sees the English language as a means to find better jobs and earn more money (Chavez 1992). In most cases, people move from one country to another because they cannot have in their own land such things as family security and social mobility (Monsivais 1995). In the new country, they change not only in reference to the conditions they left behind but also in response to the situation they propose to enter. Language is a way of bridging the distance between "us" and "them."

METHODS

Interviews were conducted between March 1998 and July 1999 with migrant workers of Mexican descent and with several informants involved in community work at the local level. The migrant workers interviewed were all Spanish-speaking adults, and their children varied as to country of origin (i.e., some were born in Mexico, others in the United States). We conducted a total of thirty-six individual, in-depth interviews, twenty-four of them with migrants. A principal aim of the interviews was to identify the difficulties and needs that developed while migrant workers resided in North Carolina. After obtaining an individual's permission, we taped the interviews (some were recorded by hand). The anonymity of all participants has been maintained.

Participants in our research reside in two distinct regions of North Carolina: the northeastern tobacco belt and the northern and central sections of the Piedmont. A snowball sampling technique was used to identify participants, as this method is particularly well suited to discovering linkages among participants (Bernard 1995). Data were obtained through a formal, open-ended questionnaire. The migrant interviews were conducted in Spanish, while interviews with nonmigrant cultural brokers were conducted primarily in English, depending on the preference of the interviewee. Interviews ranged in length from thirty minutes to three hours. Whenever possible, the interviews were conducted in the migrants' homes and at times and dates convenient to them. Interview topics included migration patterns, length of residence in the local community, employment opportunities, level of education, family size, household composition, perceptions of change within the community, and the nature of the workplace. We emphasized the investigation of the particular obstacles encountered when moving out of agriculture and into other employment sectors. We asked migrants to tell us about the needs they experienced during this transition, and to identify the services available to them to meet those needs. The most frequently cited needs were in the areas of education (including the learning of English), employment, health care, and housing.

MIGRANTS' NEEDS AND THE EDUCATIONAL SYSTEM

Spanish-speaking families find themselves in the middle of several political, cultural, and ideological battles regarding the nature and purpose of their children's education (Duignan and Gann 1998). The interviews indicated that interactions between Spanish-speaking parents and English-speaking educators had to be accomplished mostly through cultural brokers. In one community, several parents mentioned the assistance provided to them by a local bilingual teacher. The parents said they needed the most help with the mechanics of getting their children enrolled in the proper school. Since the mothers had the primary responsibility in this area, the women ended up having considerable contact with community agencies and seemed to have a heightened awareness of the desirability of English language proficiency.

Parents expressed frustration in dealing with the educational system, especially when their children attended schools that lacked the resources to bridge the language gap. Parents were willing to become involved in their children's education, but they faced many obstacles, such as the absence of bilingual teachers, the inability to communicate with teachers regarding children's academic progress, not being able to attend school meetings and activities (due to conflicting work schedules or lack of transportation or child care), and being unable to understand school correspondence sent home with the children.

Parents were also frustrated by their own educational limitations; they described themselves as being intimidated by the educational system even when language assistance was available. The parents were often unable to figure out how to navigate the system, and in many cases they lacked the academic skills needed to assist the children with their homework. They often felt impotent as they observed their children having difficulties at school and with the language in general. According to the parents, younger children were able to adjust to the school routine, but they struggled with the educational demands placed on them.

Despite these difficulties, parents acknowledged the importance of their children's education, commenting that they wanted their children to do well in school because education was the key to a better future. Among families with children, education was cited as the main reason for dropping out of migrant farmwork—it was considered important to minimize the effects of constant change in location so that the children could get a more consistent education.

Adults had their own educational needs, although these were typically utilitarian. Women in particular were interested in learning how to drive, since they believed that this skill would allow them a degree of independence when looking for work and interacting with others in the community. One female migrant worker said, "Yes, getting my driver's license is the main thing one needs. One needs to mobilize oneself here." The adults were also interested in English classes, although they were not always able to find out where the classes were held. In some cases, they did know about classes being held in local churches or community colleges, but they lacked the transportation to get to the classes or were too exhausted after work to attend. Some people attempted self-study programs, using tapes and books at home, but those whose reading and writing skills were poor even in Spanish were unable to make much progress.

MIGRANTS' NEEDS AND EMPLOYMENT OPPORTUNITIES

In his study of undocumented immigrants, Chavez (1992) notes that most of the available jobs are for unskilled or semi-skilled workers, pay minimum wages, and offer few benefits. If the immigrants remained in the United States for any length of time, however, they were usually able to find better-paying jobs with more benefits. These conditions seem to apply to the members of our study population as well.

The majority of participants in our project came to the United States in search of economic betterment. One of our informants said, "Many people, well, we all come here to this country to progress and to make more money, or to earn more money." In order to make this goal a reality, immigrants had to find employment of some sort as soon as possible upon arrival. Everyone we interviewed, however, expressed a desire to return to Mexico to live and work. One worker told us, "We have been planning to return to Mexico within the next three years so that we can work together in our own business." One could improve one's economic position much more rapidly in the United States than in Mexico, but the gains made in this country were intended to support an eventual return to Mexico.

Most of the people interviewed for this project originally came to North Carolina to work in agriculture. The majority of the men were recruited to work in the tobacco industry by either formal or informal labor agreements. Women also worked in agriculture, usually with the same farmers who employed their husbands. Their positions, however, were usually not the result of formal contracts. Some of the workers had previous experience in agriculture back in Mexico, and they found it relatively easy to adjust to conditions in North Carolina. But even those without such work experience were able to rely on other Spanish-speaking crewmates for instructions and guidance about how to proceed with the job.

Migrants who are considering residing year-round in the United States usually try to find off-farm employment (e.g., in restaurants, factories, or warehouses) during the winter months. Those in our sample who eventually left agriculture altogether mentioned the instability of that line of work, low wages, lack of benefits, and difficult health conditions as the main reasons for their decision. When migrant workers relocate off-farm, they face increased financial responsibilities, particularly after the arrival of additional family members. They would therefore prefer to find year-round employment in construction, plumbing, landscaping, manufacturing, warehousing, or retail activities. Some immigrants had used the services of employment agencies, although many relied on informal word-of-mouth networks. The majority of women worked in manufacturing or became involved in home-based activities such as child care or domestic service.

Families occasionally suffered periods of unemployment, particularly if they came into rural areas either too early or too late in the season to work in tobacco. Migrants who work through the harvest season often compromise their chances of finding factory work after the season's end, and since factory work is considered highly desirable, migrants are increasingly limiting their agricultural work. Nevertheless, once agriculture ceases to be the main source of income, workers are often unable to secure reliable transportation. They are also often hindered by a lack of telephone service. Even those immigrants in the sample who had phones were sometimes stymied by their inability to communicate in English to prospective employers.

Language emerged as a crucial factor in attaining better-paying jobs and in securing year-round employment. The majority of participants in our survey did not fully understand instructions given to them in English, and they commented that at work they relied on hand signals, demonstrations, and the assistance of translators. Often the translators were just other workers whose own English skills were not very good, and people reported feeling frustrated that much of what they needed to communicate was lost in the process. A few felt that their lack of English resulted in their being discriminated against, since those who spoke English well seemed to be given preferential treatment. Immigrants with poor English skills felt themselves to be "outsiders," but even when they knew they were being unfairly criticized, they did not know how—or even whether—to respond. Some migrants felt that their legal status left them without much recourse in the face of injustice, although many suffered from the mere fact of not really knowing what their legal rights were. Even if there was no overt discrimination, many of the migrants said that the language barrier meant that there could be no real "community" established in the workplace between Anglos and themselves.

MIGRANTS' NEEDS AND ACCESS TO HOUSING

Chavez (1992) discusses in detail the poor living conditions of migrant workers in northern San Diego County, California. They are attracted to the area by the demand for labor in the fields, but they usually end up living in makeshift campsites in discarded cardboard or plastic shelters. The conditions described by our participants are far less dramatic, but the condition of the housing they are able to secure for themselves is still very poor. Over time, a few of our participants have been able to move out of the agricultural field camps and into reasonably adequate housing, but most of them still live in substandard housing.

On-farm housing may be available for single workers arriving in North Carolina. Migrant farmworkers tend to live inside work camps; such housing usually consists of trailers, old farmhouses, or retooled tobacco sheds. These places are typically overcrowded, but they are, at least, affordable, especially since they allow for the sharing of expenses among the residents. The housing situation becomes less certain once a migrant decides to leave the farm, or once family members relocate and join the migrant worker. A noncontract migrant worker who is laboring less than full-time for the farmer increases his or her chances of being asked to leave the camp. The farmer may decide to evict a part-time worker and his or her family when additional space is needed to accommodate full-time workers, who, in most cases, are young, male, and unaccompanied. In some ways, it might be considered a positive step to leave the all-male, crowded farm camp, but doing so has the disadvantage of forcing the worker to search for scarce, affordable housing.

Finding housing in rural communities is difficult under any circumstances, as such areas rarely have large apartment complexes, trailer parks, or other rental units. The housing shortage is acute in the summer months, when the countryside is filled with extra waves of migrants. Even when housing is found, it tends to be expensive relative to the wages earned and in poor condition. Many of the people we interviewed reported that they had rented places without heating systems or running hot water. They had to rely on portable heaters and heavy blankets during the winter. Other units had defective plumbing and appliances, and some lacked functioning toilet facilities. In addition to the rent, the workers have to pay security deposits and utility fees; those who have always lived on farms may be surprised that such additional fees are always part of the bargain when one rents housing. In order to cope with the increased financial burdens, several families or multiple working adults may live together.

MIGRANTS' NEEDS AND ACCESS TO HEALTH CARE

Next to employment and housing, health-related concerns loom large in the lives of the migrants, especially those with children or pregnant women. Our interviews indicate that there are several impediments to seeking medical assistance. It can be difficult just to find out where to go for care; even if one knows where to go, it could be difficult to find transportation. Our discussions about health care focused on children's vaccinations and school physicals, childhood illnesses, prenatal and gynecological care, dental and eye exams, and work-related problems (e.g., injuries, fungal infections, contact dermatitis, green tobacco sickness).

The inability to communicate clearly with health professionals was seen as a formidable obstacle. Cultural brokers serving as translators sometimes minimized this problem, but some of the migrants seemed unconvinced that the translators were doing a good job of getting their points across. The language barrier seemed particularly difficult for women undergoing prenatal or gynecological exams; not being able to communicate directly with the professionals left them frustrated, lacking in *confianza* (trust). Women were often unhappy that the only translator available was a male, which made the already difficult process of the exam even more embarrassing.

Migrant workers come from a cultural tradition in which folk remedies are employed before one consults with a health care professional. Some people see the folk tradition as a positive thing, while others rely on such remedies only to put off the cost of going to the doctor and paying for expensive prescription medications.

Depending on migrants' residency or citizenship status, it may be possible for some to qualify for programs such as Medicare or Medicaid, especially if they are employed outside agriculture. Workers, particularly those on temporary assignments, may not be able to afford private insurance or may not qualify for health coverage at work. On the other hand, workers and their families who opt to remain in one area for an extended period of time may become ineligible to participate in local programs designed to assist migrant workers. Health-related concerns, including the language barrier, add an element of frustration and fear to already delicate and stressful situations.

LANGUAGE: A SURVIVAL TOOL FOR MIGRANTS

The element that seems to link all the different needs discussed above is English language proficiency. Regardless of the issue being discussed, language usually came up in the interviews. Migrant workers in our study made several basic connections with respect to language as a means to attain socioeconomic advancement and to build community. Migrants commented on their lack of English as a major problem as they maneuvered through a new cultural setting. Not being able to communicate in English was seen as a major obstacle, even in cases when workers knew they would be returning to Mexico one day. An everyday task back home, such as purchasing groceries, seems to require an unnecessary amount of fear and apprehension in the new rural community where the majority of residents are monolingual speakers of English.

Attempts at overcoming the language barrier take many forms. We have mentioned the assistance provided by bilingual cultural brokers. In addition, parents sometimes make use of their children's language skills, although this strategy can also create additional intergenerational conflict. Acting as interpreters can sometimes place children in difficult situations, such as having to translate for their mothers during gynecological exams. Reliance on the children also inverts the normal parent-child role relationship, contributing to parents' feelings of alienation and loss of power and exposing children to situations that may not be appropriate for their age or level of maturity.

Nevertheless, even the presence of a qualified and willing translator will not solve all problems. Some workers resent their dependence on interpreters, and others experience real anxiety about never knowing exactly what is being said. Still others complain that they can never express themselves fully as long as their most complex thoughts must always be routed through an intermediary.

In a show of self-reliance, some migrant workers have attempted to learn English at home, using tapes and books available at the local Hispanic grocery store. Others feel that they benefited from increased contact with their English-speaking neighbors and made special efforts to seek out interactions with their neighbors or at work. Formal English courses are available, although not always convenient. Some local businesses have seen the need to provide their Spanish-speaking employees with means to improve their English and so have begun offering courses at the workplace ("Compañía Manufacturera" 1998a).

The migrants in our sample also noted that overcoming the language barrier is an important way to improve their personal situations. They recognize that their children's education and language abilities will probably translate into better opportunities in the future, but they also believe that acquiring English could help them at work right now. They would like to reduce their reliance on third parties (some of whom charge a fee for their services) and increase their ability to understand the inner workings of various social and economic systems.

CONCLUSIONS

Our findings suggest that language, in this case English, is not necessarily a tool for oppression in the acculturation-assimilation context, but rather a tool for survival. The desire to acquire English proficiency was strongly supported by those we interviewed in two different Hispanic communities in North Carolina. The people to whom we spoke perceive English as a way to do better at work and at school. The ability to communicate with one's neighbors, coworkers, and employers provides a sense of belonging in a community. The ability to participate in the daily round of community life would make the migrants less "invisible" to the mainstream.

REFERENCES

Alba, R., and V. Nee. 1997. Rethinking Assimilation Theory for a New Era of Immigration. *International Migration Review* 31:826–74.

Barrera, M. 1988. *Beyond Aztlan: Ethnic Autonomy in Comparative Perspective*. New York: Praeger.

Bernard, H. 1995. *Research Methods in Anthropology: Qualitative and Quantitative Approaches. 2d ed.* Walnut Creek, Calif.: AltaMira.

Chavez, L. 1992. *Shadowed Lives: Undocumented Immigrants in American Society*. Ft. Worth, Texas: Harcourt College.

Compañía Manufacturera de Uniformes CINTAS Provee Clases Gratuitas de Inglés a sus Empleados Hispanos. 1998. *Qué Pasa Carolina* (Hispanic newspaper), October 7, 2A.

De Wind, J., and P. Kasinitz. 1997. Everything Old Is New Again? Processes and Theories of Immigrant Incorporation. *International Migration Review* 31:1096–112.

Duignan, P., and L. Gann. 1998. *The Spanish Speakers in the United States: A History.* Lanham, Md.: University Press of America.

Hispanic Populace Doubles in North Carolina. 1998. *Charlotte News and Record*, September 5, B2.

Monsivais, C. 1995. Dreaming of Utopia. *Report on the Americas* 29:39–41.

Murphy, R. 1989. *Cultural and Social Anthropology: An Overture.* Englewood Cliffs, N.J.: Prentice-Hall.

National Agricultural Workers Survey. 1997. Raleigh: North Carolina Employment Security Commission.

North Carolina Farmworker Health Alliance (NCFHA). 1996. *Facts about North Carolina's Migrant Farm Workers.* Raleigh: NCFHA.

Skerry, P. 1993. *Mexican Americans: The Ambivalent Minority.* Cambridge: Harvard University Press.

U.S. Department of Agriculture. 1998. *North Carolina Fact Sheet.* Washington, D.C.: Economic Research Service.

U.S. Department of Commerce. 1998. *Statistical Abstract of the United States.* Washington, D.C.: Bureau of the Census.

Immigration and the Organization of the Onshore Oil Industry: Southern Louisiana in the Late 1990s

Katherine M. Donato, Carl L. Bankston, and Dawn T. Robinson

Since the 1980s, the United States has experienced rising levels of new immigrants in rural areas. Large immigrant communities have appeared in locations far from the old urban centers of American immigrant life. Outside of New Orleans, Louisiana, has not in the past been a common destination for immigrants to the United States, but many Latino migrants are reportedly now working in shipbuilding and fabrication yards in coastal areas of the state. This essay is part of a larger project on differences in the adaptation and immigration of immigrants to coastal communities in southern Louisiana (Donato 1998); here we draw upon interview data from employers and community leaders to examine the employment of immigrants in the Louisiana oil industry.

The larger project covers four parishes (equivalent to counties) in southern Louisiana (Iberia, St. Mary, Terrebonne, and Lafourche), but this essay focuses on interview data from about 60 conversations in St. Mary Parish, which is situated in the middle of the Louisiana coastline. It is predominantly rural but contains a small urban center and a disproportionate share of the oil and related service industry. Our project data derive from guided conversations with a total of 270 community leaders, employers, and immigrants.

THE SOCIAL DIVISION OF LABOR IN THE OIL INDUSTRY

Dual economy studies demonstrate that labor markets may fall into one of three sectors: core, periphery, and state. Each is largely determined by the characteristics of the industries seeking workers (Bridges and Villemez 1991; Edwards 1979; Weakliem 1990). The two private segments, the core and the periphery, concern us here. The core, or the primary labor market, is found in the petroleum, auto production, and primary metal production industries (Beck, Horan, and Tolbert 1978; Tolbert, Horan, and Beck 1980). The periphery, or secondary labor market, includes industries such as seasonal agriculture, small-scale sales, textile production, and restaurants (Tolbert, Horan, and Beck 1980). Peripheral industries are volatile and are the locus of low-paid and easily discarded workers (Edwards 1979).

Many recent studies have suggested that older core-periphery distinctions are beginning to blur (Ritzer 1989). New technologies have created greater distinctions between core-sector information workers and blue-collar workers (Reich 1983). The increasingly global scale of U.S. industry means that businesses participate more in global markets and draw on a more diverse supply of workers than they did in the past; they do so either through labor migration or by relocating production in comparatively low-income countries. One consequence of this trend is that new forms of peripheral labor have appeared with increasing frequency in core industries.

ORGANIZATIONAL CHARACTERISTICS OF THE INDUSTRY

Organizational approaches to labor markets examine the characteristics of firms and establishments and how they affect the ways in which labor markets are organized (Snipp and Bloomquist 1989). Key organizational attributes are size and growth, both linked in a straightforward, positive way to the development of internal labor markets. A third attribute, unionization, is also related to internal labor market development, although this relationship is complex and not necessarily positive. Finally, the presence of certain production technologies, if they are highly specialized and require on-the-job training not transferable to other workplaces, is likely to lead to the development of an internal labor market.

Firms in different sectors have different types of organizational characteristics. In theory, core-sector industries are generally large, are more likely than peripheral industries to be unionized, and often use highly specialized production technologies. As a result, they maintain a highly skilled labor force, no matter how high the costs. In practice, however, the relationship between organizational structure and employment is complex. Often core-sector businesses often also need to rely on low-skilled peripheral labor, especially in contexts in which there is economic volatility, a factor that makes the flexibility of workers more valuable to employers than their stability.

For small employers in businesses requiring skilled workers, the costs of importing labor may often be prohibitive. Although they rely on skilled craftspeople, small employers may focus on training and retaining workers rather than importing them. Through good times and bad, small firms must provide enough incentives to workers to keep them. The modern oil industry, with its pipeline networks, crew boats, and floating hotels, is a patchwork of firms, some large and highly organized, some small and relatively informal. Coexisting alongside each other, these employers will rely on a variety of labor pools for different reasons.

LABOR MARKET ECOLOGY OF THE INDUSTRY

Labor market ecology refers to how labor markets are spatially organized and how this spatial organization helps us understand social relationships and vice versa (Horan and Tolbert 1984). Although the oil industry has become increasingly globalized, it is also locally specific in a way that other core industries are not because offshore oil structures occupy specific locations. As a result, onshore support activities, such as pipeline maintenance, building of platforms and ships, and crew boat maintenance all have to be located in the region of the oil activity. In this case, labor must go to the jobs rather than jobs to labor.

Moreover, workers who arrive in a region specifically for the purpose of work tend to come without families. In male-dominated activities of the oil business, labor migrants are primarily single men. This demographic fact affects local communities in many ways. Finding enough housing to accommodate large numbers of foreign single men is a challenge for most localities, leading to distinctive patterns of spatial distribution of immigrants.

FINDINGS

Our interviews with employers indicate that the use of immigrant labor in this Louisiana county is best understood in terms of the interrelated concepts of the changing social division of labor, organizational characteristics, and labor market ecology. Morgan City, the center of the oil industry in St. Mary Parish, lies in the southernmost region of the central part of western Louisiana, bordering the Gulf of Mexico. Employment in the area has increasingly become industrial, with petroleum mining at its center. Although St. Mary had a strong agricultural economy (especially sugar cane farming) in the past, the parish has been much more heavily involved in petroleum extraction than has the state as a whole.

In the mid-1980s, the price of oil fell drastically, and mining employment consequently declined in St. Mary Parish. By 1986, total employment had also declined considerably, since the economy of the parish was heavily dependent on jobs in the oil industry. As that industry began to rebound in the late 1980s and 1990s, many workers found jobs in a manufacturing sector driven by new oil activity.

These changes in the oil industry led to a number of other events related to the social division of labor. After the drop in oil prices in the 1980s, many highly skilled workers moved away to new markets, leaving many unskilled workers. With business connections to other geographic areas and a demand for skilled labor, some employers began to import Mexican labor from the Rio Grande Valley in the 1990s. One employer of nearly 200 workers, almost all of whom were Mexican, described the demand for foreign labor in this way: "In the past probably about two years ago, because the demand was so high, we haven't found local people. We couldn't get the black and white locals to do the work, and like most people around here, we had to concentrate heavier on foreigners."

Many immigrant employers had pre-existing connections to Texas, and its large Latino population enabled companies to draw on a Spanish-speaking labor pool. One employer told us that "companies like ourselves, we have roots in Texas, so we pull these guys out [of there]. Let's say, for instance, if Houston is having a slowdown, that's a big base of labor force to pull from, that's 3 million plus people." Once companies began hiring Latinos, they found it to be an effective way to meet their demand for skilled labor, and employers began to hire recruiters to seek out Mexican workers. One of these recruiters, who was himself of Hispanic background and spoke Spanish, explained, "I'm originally from Texas and actually I came out here to help them out with the [language]."

As skilled craftspeople, immigrant workers were employed in core occupations, and they were fairly well paid, with wages that averaged $9 to $14 per hour, frequently with free housing. They lived, however, in crowded trailer parks and had jobs that might end on short notice—both conditions are reminiscent of the situation of migrant farm workers and both are attributes of peripheral sector jobs. In addition, although immigrants have skilled occupations, they do most of the low-wage contract jobs. They also perform some of the dirtiest and least pleasant jobs that workers with these skills do, and they are conspicuous as welders and fitters in the shipbuilding and ship repair sectors. Field reports suggest that ship repair is considered an especially dirty job for skilled workers. One employer's opinion was typical. Ship repair, he told us, "is real dirty. You got to go in dirty tanks, not safe to breathe all that stuff that's in there, you know. You go in there, you cut out metal without ventilation. You are mainly dragging your butt around the shipyard, you are getting dirty." This employer later said that a shipyard job is the worst job for a welder.

Understanding how immigrant labor is part of a changing division of labor in the oil industry is only part of the picture. The demand for migrant labor is also linked to specific types of organizations. Immigrant workers are not evenly distributed among employers of all sizes. The largest employer in the area reported few immigrant workers. Although some suggest that the company has occasionally used Hispanic contract labor, this employer is considerably larger than others in the area and offers the traditional advantages of core companies: high salaries and good benefits. Both the employer and others described their jobs as the most preferred and desirable in the area because laborers usually work indoors on clean new construction. Recently, however, some have reported that the company now relies more on immigrant contract laborers, as the price of oil has dropped and volatility in the industry has risen again.

Large employers (i.e., those reporting at least 10 but fewer than 1,000 workers) are also the biggest employers of Latino workers. These employers have the financial and organizational resources to recruit and house immigrant workers. One official from a smaller company described how larger businesses tend to take in the immigrants. "They brought up about 200 people and they were feeding them, giving them living quarters, transporting to and from work locations." Such measures were too expensive for his own small company.

All the large companies in our sample rely on immigrants as welders and fitters, although none of the small employers hired migrant labor. This finding was surprising, in that we expected small businesses, which are traditionally found in the peripheral sector, to attract migrants. But smaller employers actually depend on a stable rather than flexible labor force because they are disadvantaged when seeking labor. They also pursue this strategy because the smaller the company, the more closely the employees have to work together, and the more important it is to maintain good communications and good relations. Therefore, people from outside the region who cannot speak English are often seen as poor choices for small employers. They fit better in larger work settings, where expansion and contraction are common, depending on economic trends.

Unable to find sufficient qualified workers, some medium- and large-sized employers began busing in groups of Latinos from South Texas during the mid-1990s. Large groups of single men, speaking little English and arriving together in a geographically constrained community, attracted more attention and concern than isolated individuals finding slots in the local economy. Employers faced the difficulty of finding housing for their imported work crews. Trailers, cheap and portable, seemed to offer the answer. One of the employers explained this decision: "Basically in South Louisiana there is pretty much little or no housing available. We did a study a while back of mobile homes in the South Louisiana area. Terrebonne Parish, for example, has gone from 30 to the neighborhood of 250 [mobile home] permits per week. It is a cheap, quick way to set up housing."

In the late summer of 1997, immigrant workers became a major source of controversy in Morgan City. One shipbuilding firm, which employed a total of 200 workers, had begun to employ many immigrants who were housed in fifteen trailers on commercial property owned by the firm. This situation drew complaints from residents of a nearby neighborhood, who accused the firm of violating a zoning ordinance. By September, charges were lodged against the company for being slow in moving the trailers; three additional employers were cited for lodging immigrant workers on their property. The human resources director at the first company told us that he felt that cultural and linguistic fears stood behind objections to the trailers. "The biggest problem in the local community we see," he said, "is the people don't work twenty-four hours around the day. They have time off and lack of things to do and places to go. The lack of communication skills, with the local people, does create a lot of problems in the community [like] tension, spitefulness. Some local people see the foreigners coming in and taking American jobs."

In response to the public outrage, the owner of a ship repair company arranged to move the trailers to property in Amelia, a small town just outside Morgan City. Amelia is a relatively new community, consisting of only a few houses in the 1970s. Its growth came as a response to the oil activities of the late 1970s and early 1980s, as job seekers began showing up in the Morgan City area looking for cheap housing. At that time, the low-income housing available in Amelia was attracting many of the 1,000 Vietnamese refugees who settled in the community. Specializing first in fishing and shrimping, and later going into oil-related occupations, the Vietnamese have begun to achieve upward mobility, and by the late 1990s they owned most of the convenience stores in town.

This confluence of events has created an interesting social and economic ecology in Amelia. Most stores in this little town are owned by Vietnamese, and their customers are mainly Hispanic workers. The two groups do not otherwise socialize with each other or even attend the same church. When asked how Hispanic workers were integrating into the life of the community, one of our respondents observed that "They don't like to venture out and mingle but they kind of isolate themselves."

This geographic concentration and isolation suggests that although Latino workers are engaged in mainstream economic activities and have some impact on local businesses, they are peripheral to the social life of the area. Aside from patronizing convenience stores and inexpensive food establishments, though, the single male immigrant workers do not have much effect on the community—they are "simply sending money back home," according to one employer.

CONCLUSIONS

Small towns in Louisiana are not often considered a hub of international migration. We have seen, however, that recent developments in the offshore oil industry have produced demands for a variety of onshore commodities and services. As a result, by the 1990s, the production of onshore commodities and services was drawing a large, primarily Latino immigrant labor force. Our field research in Morgan City, a center of onshore oil activity, has identified a number of dimensions of immigrant labor in the region.

Events in the oil industry shaped the social division of labor in Morgan City. The area's heavy dependence on oil made it the site of blue-collar, industrial jobs. The close linkage between the local economy and world oil prices meant that the local economy was uncertain and unstable, qualities that both exacerbated labor shortages in good times and created a need for a flexible work force. The globalization of Morgan City is consistent with developments in other industries in the United States, where increasing connections to worldwide markets in labor and resources are encouraging flexibility among American workers. These same trends also often result in production itself moving abroad, which is not, however, an option in the oil industry, since firms that service that industry must be located in proximity to the oil production itself. Immigration to Louisiana therefore differs from labor movement trends in Mexico, where employers tend to locate near large pools of labor. In our case study, foreign workers are coming to the employers, no matter how remote or nontraditional the destination may seem.

The connection to international labor has blurred many of the traditional distinctions between core and peripheral sectors. Immigrant workers in southern Louisiana are skilled craftsmen, not migrant farm workers, day laborers, or dishwashers. At the same time, however, older divisions of labor associated with core and periphery sectors have not been entirely abandoned. Latino laborers made up the bulk of the contract workers in the area, and even though Hispanic welders, fitters, and carpenters were relatively well paid, they frequently performed some of the dirtiest jobs possible.

The blurring of core and peripheral attributes was also seen in the organizational characteristics related to immigrant employment. Fairly large, stable businesses became those most likely to import workers, just as large automobile manufacturers (another traditional core industry in the United States) were among the firms most likely to establish foreign production. Larger businesses could afford the costs of recruiting foreign workers and relied less on employee loyalty and communication with and among employees, as compared with the smaller firms.

Finally, the spatial ecology of migrant labor in southern Louisiana illustrated how this new type of labor is organized. Latino workers not only fill specific occupational niches; they also have come to settle in residential niches. Geographically, linguistically, and socially isolated, these immigrants have become a major part of the labor force in the Morgan City area, but they have seldom mingled with others and have sent most of their earnings home to Texas or Mexico. Since the initial controversy over housing Mexicans in trailers on commercial property, immigrant workers have become virtually invisible. We suggest that an internal *maquiladora* has developed and has made profits for U.S. businesses while existing outside the consciousness of most Americans.

NOTE

An earlier version of this paper was presented at the 1999 annual meeting of the Southern Anthropological Society in Decatur, Georgia. We gratefully acknowledge support from Minerals Management Service at the U.S. Department of the Interior and contributions from the graduate students on this project, Melissa Stainback and Patricia Campion.

REFERENCES

Beck, E., P. Horan, and C. Tolbert. 1978. Stratification in a Dual Economy: A Structural Model of Earnings Determination. *American Sociological Review* 43:704–20.

Bridges, W., and W. Villemez. 1991. Employment Relations and the Labor Market: Integrating Institutional and Labor Market Perspectives. *American Sociological Review* 56:748–64.

Donato, K. 1998. *Labor Migration and the Deepwater Oil Industry*. Washington, D.C.: U.S. Department of the Interior.

Edwards, R. 1979. *Contested Terrain*. New York: Basic Books.

Horan, P., and C. Tolbert. 1984. *The Organization of Work in Rural and Urban Labor Markets*. Boulder, Colo.: Westview.

Reich, R. 1983. *The Next American Frontier*. New York: Times Books.

Ritzer, G. 1989. The Permanently New Economy: The Case for Reviving Economic Sociology. *Work and Occupations* 16:243–72.

Snipp, C., and L. Bloomquist. 1989. Sociology and Labor Market Structure: A Selective Overview. *Research in Rural Sociology and Development* 4:1–27.

Tolbert, C., P. Horan, and E. Beck. 1980. The Structure of Economic Segmentation: A Dual Economy Approach. *American Journal of Sociology* 85:1095–116.

Weakliem, D. 1990. Relative Wages and the Radical Theory of Economic Segmentation. *American Sociological Review* 55:574–90.

Heading South: Why Mexicans and Mexican-Americans in Brownsville, Texas, Cross the Border into Mexico

Kathleen M. Murphy

From the way immigration is represented in the media, one would be tempted to conclude that Mexicans only travel northward. Mexicans are often characterized as a threat to the United States, and the presumed effects of their presence have provoked various xenophobic responses. The supposed linguistic threat has encouraged an "English first" movement, and perceived economic threats have led to legislative restrictions on government benefits paid to recent immigrants.[1]

But what about people heading south? This paper offers some preliminary analysis of patterns of southerly border crossing and migration among Mexican nationals and Mexican-Americans living in Brownsville, Texas. I also offer some interpretive comments about the relationship between these crossings and processes of identity formation in the border communities.

NOTES ON THE METHOD

The empirical basis of this report is the set of transcripts of interviews with fifteen low-income households that my colleague Cathy Jackson conducted in 1997.[2] I also draw on conversations I had during fourteen household interviews conducted in Matamoros, Mexico, several months earlier, as well as on my participant observation in Brownsville. In addition to using the "snowball" method, we got in touch with these particular families through people we knew on both sides of the border who worked in a variety of governmental, nongovernmental, and religious agencies in Matamoros and Brownsville. We also were assisted by colleagues at the Colegio de la Frontera Norte in Matamoros. No more than two contacts, however, were used from each source, nor did we interview more than two households in any given *colonia* (neighborhood) or housing development.

All twenty-nine households included dependent children. It was the senior female of the home who usually granted the interview, which lasted between two and five hours, spaced out over at least two visits that might vary in intervals of a few days or a few weeks. Questions were open-ended, and conversational topics included the family's background, household formation and composition, and why the family lived in a particular *colonia*. More detailed questions elicited quantitative data about household expenses, how families cut corners to save money, and what household members were doing or had done to earn incomes. We also asked about patterns of child care, the state of each household member's health (both physical and mental), the stresses of material hardship, and how they felt overall about their current situations and their hopes for the future.

AN OVERVIEW OF BORDER-CROSSING

These conversations help us understand why the people with whom we talked voluntarily crossed the border into Mexico; we also briefly consider forced departures. The crossings may be associated with either short-term visits or residential moves. Short-term visits to Matamoros were made to consult with Mexican physicians, to purchase or sell goods, and to visit family members or participate in broader social networks, or some combination of all these factors. For example, someone who attends a Mexican medical clinic or sees a doctor might also do a bit of shopping while there, and as I argue, the consumption of such goods and services is a means of producing identities. People moved to Mexico for a variety of reasons, such as the need to make use of land owned in Mexico, but many of the respondents chose not to elaborate on their reasons.

Involuntary departures involve deportations, which have increased all along the U.S.-Mexico border due to *la migra* (the Immigration and Naturalization Service, or INS) since 1996, when the Illegal Immigration Reform and Immigrant Responsibility act (IIRIRA) was approved.[3]

None of the people in our survey, however, reported deportations since the passage of the law, although a climate of fear was apparent during our conversations. Their concern was also due to welfare reform and the effect of cutbacks on recent immigrants.[4] I expect that as research continues, it will become more important to consider carefully how welcome someone felt in the United States before deciding to move south.

SHORT-TERM VISITS TO MATAMOROS: VISITING THE DOCTOR OR PHARMACIST

Six of the fifteen households in Brownsville had someone who went to Matamoros for health-related reasons. In one case, it was to purchase anti-depressants available at relatively low cost. Others relied on Mexican doctors as their primary physicians, especially those who had lived in Matamoros at one time; some also maintained ongoing relationships with dentists. Some people use both the U.S. and Mexican health care systems, alternating to save money or to get second opinions.[5] One woman exemplifies the "push-pull" nature of motivation; she is drawn to the doctors in Matamoros for their expertise, but she also felt dissatisfied with the care in the United States and had to fight to get coverage. She says:

> My oldest daughter, she has lupus. You know what that is? She has that. And she has days when she feels good and days when she doesn't. And my other daughter, she had a brain tumor. She had a tumor in the brain. And I worry a lot about that. And my son he also has a tumor in his arm. And then one of my grandsons, he has stomach pains. But the doctors cannot find anything. Here the doctors say that they don't know what it is. And we went to Matamoros, as best as I could got money for X-rays. They are giving me Medicaid through welfare. And for my oldest daughter I was fighting, since she is already eighteen years, they took it away from her. They just gave her disability this past year. They gave her disability this past November. This past year. Because she has many problems, right? And they didn't want to give her disability, right, but they had to because it has already affected her kidneys, and she's already had problems, right? And so they gave her disability, my oldest daughter. But I already want to take her

to Matamoros, to Monterrey, to other doctors, to see if they'll give her medicine, right? But I need money from my [oldest] son because everything is very expensive. I love my daughter, right, and I had help from a doctor in San Antonio in a place that works with chronic diseases. And they took both of us. And not everything was covered, right? There were certain things that were covered and certain things not, right? Like when they took away her Medicaid she had to keep checking on her heart and her brain but that wasn't covered.

Many of our respondents preferred medical care in Mexico, but even if they did not, they had no affordable option in the United States.[6]

SHORT-TERM VISITS: CONSUMPTION AND THE PRODUCTION OF IDENTITY

Another frequently cited reason to cross the border was to consume Mexican goods. People reported buying gas, cigarettes, cleaning items, and clothing in Mexico. They also accessed certain services, such as haircuts. One couple saved money on auto registration fees by keeping their car registered in Mexico under a relative's name. People said that things in Mexico were cheaper, but I agree with Zúñiga (1998), who suggested that the consumption of certain goods and services is part of how Mexico is both imagined and experienced, and so is a part of maintaining cultural identity.

This process can occur on either side of the border. Sometimes goods are purchased in Mexico for sale in the United States. On the other hand, there was one woman who collected secondhand clothing and blankets for next-to-nothing in the United States and traveled home to sell them. When that woman returned to Brownsville, she would bring back a stock of sweets, seeds, and tostadas from Matamoros to sell to neighbors. The process of maintaining cultural identity also includes continued watching and listening to Mexican TV and radio. Limón (1998:102) quotes the lyrics of a popular *ranchera* song:

Yo soy mexicano
De acá de este lado;
De acá de este lado
Puro mexicano.

Y aunque la gente
Me llame tejano,
Yo les aseguro
Que soy mexicano,
De acá de este lado.
[I am a Mexican over here / From this side; / From this side /
Pure Mexican. / And even though people / Call me a Texan, / I
assure you / That I am Mexican, / From this side.]

As Limón (1998:102) explains, "Even though we were Texas-born and
raised and called *tejanos*, many of us—this singer-persona, my mother
and I, and his audience in Texas and beyond—were still claiming to be
puro Mexicano [pure Mexican] even though we lived on the U.S. side
of the border."

Using Mexican doctors and consuming other goods and services
within a territorial space politically marked as "Mexican" contributes
to a sense of authenticity in one's own "Mexicanidad." Ainslie
(1998:291) offers a poignant analysis of *la Pulga,* the flea market
outside of Austin, Texas, which is heavily patronized on weekends
by Mexicans who live too far from the border for a quick trip to Mexico.
In addition to goods and services that help immigrants make transitions
to life in the United States, "the numerous produce stands are indis-
tinguishable from their Mexican counterparts in terms of their selec-
tion . . . as well as in their atmosphere, creating a temporary visual/
sensual illusion that one is back home in Mexico, thereby replenishing
these immigrants via a reimmersion in the lost familiar." Those living
in Brownsville may be crossing for a similar dose of the familiar.

SHORT-TERM VISITS: VISITING FAMILY AND FRIENDS

We might note the etymological link between Ainslie's use of "familiar" and "family"; consumption of goods and services in Matamoros
was often done in the company of family and friends. These practices
sometimes led to the construction of transnational families. One thirty-
three-year-old woman was born in Tamaulipas, the fifth of seven children. When she was thirteen, her family moved to Matamoros, and she
began to work in a *maquiladora.* She gave birth at age eighteen to a
daughter, taking care of expenses herself then and throughout most of

her twenties, even though she was married between the ages of twenty and twenty-three. In her late twenties, she met her current partner, with whom she bore a baby girl, age three at the time of the interview. Since the baby's father lives and works in Brownsville, this new nuclear family moved there. The woman's fifteen-year-old daughter, however, was living with her grandparents in Matamoros so that she could finish school. Her mother went to Matamoros to visit her every two weeks.

One man moved back to Matamoros after his wife died in 1982 so that his parents could help take care of his daughters. After a year he returned to Brownsville because he wanted the girls to attend a U.S. school, and his mother would sometimes come to Brownsville to help out. His parents continued to live in Matamoros, and he visited them almost daily.

It is a commonly held idea in the United States that Mexican women consistently cross the border only to give birth. But a different scenario is illustrated by Carolina (a pseudonym), age twenty-nine, who was born in Brownsville, the youngest of four children. None of the siblings had the same father, and only one of the fathers helped her mother at all, although he is now deceased. Carolina was raised by her maternal aunt because her mother earned money selling clothes across the border. No one stopped Carolina from dropping out of the U.S. school system at age fourteen; she had been enrolled in what her mother called "special classes," which were apparently for students with learning problems. Shortly thereafter, her aunt died. One of her mother's cousins took her in; in return, Carolina was to work around the house, cooking and cleaning. Given these years of unpaid labor, Carolina has never been in the labor force. When she became pregnant in 1992, her mother was living in Mexico and encouraged Carolina to deliver the baby in Matamoros, where a friend of the family lived and could help out with the delivery. Since this little girl was not born in the United States and lived in Matamoros until age two, when Carolina moved back to Brownsville, the child's citizenship papers had not been processed, and she was not eligible for Medicaid. Carolina had been told by her social worker that there was a fee to process the papers, but she could not afford it. Carolina's move back to Brownsville coincided with the birth of her son, which Medicaid did cover.[7]

In Carolina's case, then, we see an unfortunate result: because she relied on social networks in Mexico, her child's access to the benefits in the United States was limited.[8] As Vélez-Ibáñez (1996:83) points out, even before the most recent and punitive immigration and welfare reform legislation was passed,

> Even within the same extended familial network the legalization of one family member sharply contrasts with the illegality of others. Together with immigration sweeps of Mexican workers [and, I would add, welfare reform's anti-immigrant provisions], which seem to coincide with immigration "reform" bills . . . further emphasis has been placed on the "foreignness" of the Mexican population in Mexico in comparison to that of the United States and on the mythic cultural differences between the populations. Such demographic and political splitting between Mexico-born and U.S.-born Mexicans establishes the cultural basis for the creation of an ethnic U.S.-Mexican and the denial of cultural continuity between separate populations.

LONGER-TERM CROSSINGS: OWNING LAND

People in Brownsville, especially those who had grown up in Mexico, talked about moving permanently to Mexico. In addition to familial ties, ownership of land could explain the strong attachment to Mexico. Other studies have noted the attachment people feel to the specific territory and community of their *pueblo*, which might become especially important during the town's annual celebration of its saint's day, as in Tehuixtla, described by Ainslie (1998:293–97). In our study, one woman and her partner planned to stay in Brownsville only long enough to earn sufficient money to allow them to build a house on land they own in Guanajuato. He does odd jobs, and she works as a maid for a woman who lets them live in a small building on her property. Her partner had worked previously in the United States and had earned enough to buy a car. They have stayed at various times with relatives, but always in crowded, unsuitable conditions. She says:

> We bought a piece of land there [in Mexico] because [we were] renting and renting all of the time. And you know that sometimes you get tired and want your own house. And that is why we came here, as we see it, to get ahead. But we definitely see that you can't do that here. And in a year we haven't done anything. Sure,

he began to work in August. But like I said, he has weeks that he doesn't work. Week after week. It doesn't seem good to me.

Despite their desire to go back and the trouble they are having raising money for the house they would like to build back in Guanajuato, it is unlikely that they will realize their "return fantasies," a situation echoed in the research of Durand (1998), Cornelius (1998), and Suárez-Orozco (1998).

LONGER-TERM CROSSINGS: GOING HOME

Other people were less specific about why they moved to Mexico, although a combination of factors seems operative: returning to their roots and the familiar network of family and friends seemed more attractive than struggling in the United States. For example, one couple almost returned to Mexico when they were not succeeding in the United States:

> *husband:* During that period we had the money to pay the rent. For example, when we bought the trailer. But one time we had to pay 200 [dollars] for the trailer, and so I told my wife, "We can pay the 150 a month for something that can be more useful to us." And we can try to save more money in order to be able to do more things. And unfortunately that's when I found myself without a job.
> *wife:* I think that we would have decided to go to Matamoros. Because we didn't know what to do. But then we bought the trailer and we could continue to get ahead. And then he got a job.
> *husband:* Well, there wasn't a time when we didn't have money because we have always tried to plan, first the rent, before anything else one has to have someplace to live, right? And to always have money to pay for that. But because this opportunity presented itself, now we have the trailer. And we paid it a little at a time. $10 a week. Now we are getting ahead.

INVOLUNTARY DEPARTURES

While such moves back to Mexico may have been prompted by hard times, we have thus far dealt only with voluntary departures. Deportation—and fear of it—clearly increased in the 1990s. Even those who may not have direct experience with deportation could not miss the militarization of the border, although it is obvious that people cross to Mexico and manage to cross back as well. Kearney (1997:156) offers a provocative analysis of the apparent tightening of the U.S.-Mexican border. Since the border remains full of literal holes, "the surveillance activities of the Border Patrol are not intended to prevent [recent migrants'] entry into the United States to work but instead are part of a number of ways of disciplining them to work hard and to accept low wages."[9] One of the women we talked to in Brownsville describes a border that is easily crossed despite her frequent deportations. She was raised in Mexico and came to Brownsville to stay in 1962, when she was thirteen, but she often visits Matamoros. She comments: "Well, I stayed. They caught me a couple of times and sent me to Mexico, but I always came back. Before I got my residential papers I ask to write for a pardon, so they can give me my residential papers. And they forgive me so they give me my papers." Consistent with Kearney's assertion that the immigration laws promote a Foucaultian micro-discipline is the woman's description of the authorities granting her "forgiveness." But it is also worth noting that this woman's story is based primarily on crossings that occurred before the tightening of the border. However, despite Kearney's analysis, it should not be overlooked that not all border crossers survive the trek, as they go without water, skirting customs agents in the hot sun.

CONCLUDING QUALIFICATIONS

This essay considers why both Mexican nationals and Mexican-Americans living in Brownsville, Texas, choose to cross the border in a southerly direction. Its conclusions are qualified for a number of reasons. First, these are not the only groups involved, even though they were the only ones with whom interviews were conducted. It would clearly be useful to find out why other ethnic and racial groups cross into Mexico from the United States, both for purposes of comparison as well as to consider how participation in Mexican goods and services affects the production of a specific "border" identity even for presumed "Anglos," and how residents of Mexico feel about these southerly directed border crossers. Second, the data on which this discussion is based derive from a small sample and so can only suggest patterns of behavior, not quantify them. Third, as stated, the interview topics were primarily designed to elicit information about where people worked and consumed goods and services. It would take more in-depth conversation and participant observation to understand what roles family and other personal relationships played in decisions about moving back to Mexico, as well as what importance was attributed to the identification with practices of work and consumption that are specific to Mexico. These assertions are tentative and will most likely be revised as the research continues in these same communities.

NOTES

1. See Orenstein (1995) for a brief, though somewhat dated, overview of these trends. The tightening of human flows across the border has, of course, been accompanied by a relaxation of controls as they apply to business collaborations. For a site-specific example, see Martin and Cushman (1998).

2. Cathy Jackson's study, "Mexican-American Families in Border and Urban Settings: Children and Parents Making Ends Meet," was directed by Laura Lein of the Center for Social Work Research and the Department of Anthropology at the University of Texas at Austin. Funding was provided by the Hogg Foundation for Mental Health. The project also served as a pilot for ongoing research to explore the differences between the experiences of poverty on both sides of the border. This stage of the research is being conducted under a National Science Foundation grant, "Comparative Study of the Urban Poor," with Laura Lein and Henry Selby as principal investigators, in consultation with Yolanda Padilla, Manuel Ribeiro, and Eduardo López. The NSF grant will expand the scope of the research to include San Antonio and Monterrey and will provide more detail about social constructions of poverty, with particular attention to differences in the nature and degree of stigma attached to poverty and receipt of government benefits.

3. The Center for Immigration Research at the University of Houston has a team of researchers working on this and other immigration issues. Randy Capps presented their findings in El Paso on January 22, 1999, at one of the trio of conferences held during spring 1999 on border issues. The conferences, hosted by the University of Texas System and the Sistema Nacional Para el Desarrollo Integral de la Familia (DIF) dealt with the needs of Mexican nationals living in the United States. The DIF has been concerned with how to help Mexicans who are delivered by the U.S. government to Mexican border cities that are not necessarily their homes. In the absence of personal networks, they often turn to the DIF for assistance.

4. My conclusion also takes into account stories I heard while interviewing Mexican-Americans who had been refused welfare or had been discouraged from continuing with the program. At the time I was managing a project on welfare "leavers" in San Antonio.

5. De Ann Pendry is exploring this issue of dual medical care with respect to diabetes treatment. She is studying diabetes patients in San Antonio and the use they make of both Mexican and U.S. health care practitioners.

6. Laura Lein and I were in Monterrey in June 1995. Her daughter developed a sore throat and was taken to a doctor. Lein was struck by how attentive and prompt the doctor was, a style of care she believes the U.S. system makes difficult for even well-intentioned practitioners.

7. The baby's father was not aware of Carolina's pregnancy, and she has not pursued legal efforts to obtain child support from him.

8. See Brown and Wyn (1998) for further information about health insurance coverage and access to health services among Mexican-American children living in the United States, with particular attention paid to the effects of immigration status (their own as well as that of their parents).

9. Kearney offers this description of the border fence: "old, bent, and festooned with rags and scrapes [sic] of paper impaled on it by the wind. It has many gaping holes through which 'illegal' border crossers come and go almost as freely as the wind" (1997:153). See also Andreas (1998) for information about the condition of the border.

REFERENCES

Ainslie, R. 1998. Cultural Mourning, Immigration, and Engagement: Vignettes from the Mexico Experience. In *Crossings: Mexican Immigration in Interdisciplinary Perspective*, ed. M. Suárez-Orozco, 283–300. Cambridge: Harvard University Press.

Andreas, P. 1998. The U.S. Immigration Control Offensive: Constructing an Image of Order on the Southwest Border. In *Crossings: Mexican Immigration in Interdisciplinary Perspective*, ed. M. Suárez-Orozco, 341–61. Cambridge: Harvard University Press.

Brown, E., and R. Wyn. 1998. Access to Health Insurance and Health Care for Mexican-American Children in Immigrant Families. In *Crossings: Mexican Immigration in Interdisciplinary Perspective*, ed. M. Suárez-Orozco, 227–47. Cambridge: Harvard University Press.

Cornelius, W. 1998. The Structural Embeddedness of Demand for Mexican Immigrant Labor: New Evidence from California. In *Crossings: Mexican Immigration in Interdisciplinary Perspective*, ed. M. Suárez-Orozco, 113–44. Cambridge: Harvard University Press.

Durand, J. 1998. Migration and Integration: Intermarriages among Mexicans and Non-Mexicans in the United States. In *Crossings: Mexican Immigration in Interdisciplinary Perspective*, ed. M. Suárez-Orozco, 207–21. Cambridge: Harvard University Press.

Kearney, M. 1997. Borders and Boundaries of State and Self at the End of Empire. In *Migrants, Regional Identities and Latin American Cities*, ed. T. Altamirano and L. Hirabayashi, 151–68. Washington, D.C.: Society for Latin American Anthropology.

Limón, J. 1998. *American Encounters: Greater Mexico, the United States, and the Erotics of Culture*. Boston: Beacon.

Martin, S., and R. Cushman. 1998. Applying Industrial Ecology to Industrial Parks: An Economic and Environmental Analysis. *Economic Development Quarterly* 12:218–38.

Orenstein, C. 1995. Illegal Transnational Labor: Mexicans in California and Haitians in the Dominican Republic. *Journal of International Affairs* 48:601–25.

Suárez-Orozco, M. 1998. Introduction. In *Crossings: Mexican Immigration in Interdisciplinary Perspective*, ed. M. Suárez-Orozco, 3–50. Cambridge: Harvard University Press.

Vélez-Ibáñez, C. 1996. *Border Visions: Mexican Cultures of the Southwest United States*. Tucson: University of Arizona Press.

Zúñiga, V. 1998. Representaciones Infantiles de la Frontera y del Espacio Nacional. In *Voces de la Frontera: Estudios sobre la Dispersión Cultural en la Frontera México–Estados Unidos*, ed. V. Zúñiga, 221–300. Monterrey, México: Universidad Autónoma de Nuevo León.

A New Destination for an Old Migration: Origins, Trajectories, and Labor Market Incorporation of Latinos in Dalton, Georgia

Victor Zúñiga and Rubén Hernández-León

This essay presents findings of a case study that describes the social process of migration and the incorporation of Latino and Mexican immigrants to the United States into the labor market in their new destination. The study took place in Dalton, a small city in northwest Georgia, which in the 1990s experienced a great expansion of its immigrant population. We analyze Dalton's experience from two perspectives. First, this is a case study with distinctive, idiosyncratic characteristics. The city is known as the Carpet Capital of the World because it produces approximately 80 percent of all wall-to-wall carpet manufactured in the United States. For the past ten years, many Latino immigrants have settled in Dalton. The 1990 census reported the presence of 2,321 Hispanics in Whitfield County (of which Dalton is the seat), but data from the Center for Applied Research in Anthropology at Georgia State University showed that in 1997 there were more than 45,000 Hispanics in the county (Center for Applied Research in Anthropology 1998; U.S. Census Bureau 1999).

Second, we contend that Dalton is representative of a broader process of seeking new destinations for Latin American and particularly Mexican migration to the United States. In this context, the southeastern states appear to be a prominent receiving area, although new destinations also include locations in the Midwest and Northeast. How can we explain this new diaspora of the Latino population in the United States? We can understand both the spatial and temporal dimensions of this process because of the passage and implementation of the Immigration Reform and Control Act (IRCA) of 1986. The amnesty program, a central component of IRCA, allowed for the legalization of 3 million immigrants, most of whom eventually attained legal permanent resident status. Once they legalized their status, Latino immigrants have exited traditional regions and cities of destination and concentration, mainly in the Southwest, in order to search for labor markets with higher wages and less competition from persons of the same ethnicity and national origin (Durand 1998).

The arrival of Latino immigrants in these new destinations has been both recent and sudden, and therefore few studies have dealt with flows and settlements in atypical localities and regions from either a case study or a national perspective (Durand, Massey, and Charvet 1998; Gouveia and Saenz 1999; Hernández-León and Zúñiga 2000). For that reason, this essay does not address a series of research questions stemming from the literature on international migration; rather, it outlines a profile of the immigrant community of Dalton by discussing its origins, migration trajectories, and local labor market incorporation.

METHODS

This study of Dalton is part of a larger service project in which scholars and staff of the Universidad de Monterrey in Mexico designed a series of programs to assist the public schools of Dalton and Whitfield County in their efforts to respond to the needs of Spanish-speaking students. In the 1998–99 school year, 41.5 percent of the student body in the public schools of Dalton was of Hispanic origin. The inception and implementation of these programs, officially known as the Georgia Project, have been analyzed by Hamann (1999).

The research program of the Georgia Project has used multiple methodological strategies with the objective of generating in-depth, detailed knowledge about the immigrant community in Dalton. This knowledge, in turn, has been used to nourish other areas of the project. Even though we began researching the newcomer community using ethnographic methods, such as participant observation, in-depth interviews, and focus groups (Hernández-León et al. 1997), this essay is based on a survey of Latino parents whose children were enrolled in Dalton's public schools. The survey was conducted in the winter of 1997–98.

The survey process began with the compilation of a list of all the school district's matriculated students in order to identify those with Latino surnames. Once we cross-checked for siblings and pupils who had left school, we came up with a list of 958 families, although the number was reduced because some people could not be reached due to divorce, migration, or death. Bilingual Mexican teachers working in the schools handed out two written surveys in Spanish to one child in each family. One survey was to be answered by the mother and the other one by the father. A week later, these teachers collected the returned and completed questionnaires. The response rate was approximately 50 percent (49 percent for fathers and 52 percent for mothers). The final sample analyzed here is composed of 407 men and 439 women.

Given the limitations of the survey, the data presented here should be interpreted with some reservations. The sampling frame does not encompass all families of Latino origin in either Dalton or Whitfield County. Because only those families with children enrolled in Dalton's public schools were included, the sampling frame excluded from the outset those kin groups whose children already graduated, those whose offspring were not yet in school, and those whose kids were matriculated in private or county schools. Moreover, the survey did not include single individuals who might not have children but who frequently make up an important segment of an immigrant community, particularly during the early stages of its development (Massey et al. 1987). We decided to use the public schools in Dalton as the basis for a sampling frame for both practical and analytical reasons. First, given available resources, time restrictions, and existing access to immigrants, the schools were the means to the most effective collection of data about a large number of immigrants. Second, previously conducted ethnographic observations suggested that Latino migration to Dalton included many families, so that the schools represented a sample whose characteristics would resemble those of the larger population.

It is worth stressing that ours was not a random sample, so that there may be a bias inherent in the self-selection factor. This limitation is significant in that even though the questionnaire did not include questions about legal status, those who lacked documents might have been inclined not to answer. Such a reaction might have been expected given the climate of fear and state policing that many immigrant communities are now experiencing in the United States.

ORIGINS

The Latino immigrants who have settled in Dalton form a group that is highly homogeneous in terms of origins. According to our survey, 94 percent of the immigrants were born in Mexico. The non-Mexican segment of the population is composed of persons born in various southern states such as Georgia, Tennessee, and Florida (1 percent), individuals born in states outside the South, especially Texas (4 percent), and those born in Central and South America, especially Guatemala, El Salvador, Nicaragua, and Colombia (1 percent). In the case of Dalton, therefore, ethnic labels like "Latino" or "Hispanic" are virtually equivalent to "Mexican." Most of the Mexico-born respondents are originally from the central and western states (Michoacán, Jalisco, Nayarit, Guanajuato, Zacatecas, and Aguascalientes) that together form the core of the region that has historically sent the most migrants north of the border.

As noted above, immigration to Dalton has been a recent and sudden phenomenon. Our survey data indicate that almost one-third of the respondents had been in Dalton for less than three years. Only 4 percent had lived in the city for more than twelve years. The average time of residence in Dalton was 4.6 years (5.1 years for men and 4.1 years for women). Although they are new to Dalton, however, these people are not new to the migration process. Dalton is, in effect, a new destination for seasoned international migrants.

We have identified three distinct groups in the sample by using the year of first trip to the United States as the baseline for the initiation of a migratory career. First, there are pre-IRCA migrants who first arrived in the country before 1986. They make up 40 percent of the sample, they are predominantly men (only one-third are women), and almost all were born in Mexico. This is the oldest (mean age is thirty-six years) and least educated group, although it is the segment with the longest migratory experience and the greatest fluency in English. Second, there are those who arrived in the United States right after the passage of IRCA. They constitute slightly more than 25 percent of the sample and are the youngest group (average age is 31.9 years). Most of the people in this group seem to be children of older, pioneer migrants, and 14 percent of them were born in the United States. As such, they have considerably higher levels of schooling than those in the first group (an average of eight years of education). The third group consists of those who have arrived since 1991. Most of them are women (74 percent), and most of them speak only Spanish. These people migrated mostly to achieve family reunification. Men who arrived before 1986 legalized their status through IRCA's amnesty program and subsequently sent for their wives and children.

It is worth noting that the three groups are not radically different from each other in terms of the time they have lived in Dalton. In fact, the average time of residence in the city is about the same for all groups. Viewed as a whole, these migrants are recent arrivals to Dalton, but many have a long history of international migration. Their move into a new destination is part of a transformation of the geography of Mexican immigration to the United States (Hernández-León and Zúñiga 2000).

TRAJECTORIES

Analysis of our survey data allows for a partial reconstruction of the trajectories that migrants have followed to arrive at this new destination. A fuller understanding of the diversity of the trajectories could be gleaned only through extended life history methodology, so our findings are couched in terms of hypotheses for further testing, rather than as formal conclusions.

We took into account four points in the trajectories of migrants in order to depict the pathways for arrival in Dalton: place of birth, destination for the first U.S. trip, locality where the individual migrant was living immediately before moving to Dalton, and current place of residence. It is evident that this analysis cannot take into account the uncertainties of international migration, which include circular moves, deportation, numerous trips back and forth, and sudden changes in domicile. Moreover, in order to clarify our discussion, we do not consider the periods of residence in each location.

The migrants who were born in central and western Mexico tend to move to either California or Georgia as a first destination, depending on the period during which that first trip was made. Others go first to Texas and then move to Georgia or return to Mexico. The rest make an original trip to Illinois, Florida, or New York. Despite the diversity of migratory moves, however, there are three main trajectories. The first is that of those migrants who move directly to Georgia, return to Mexico, and then come back to Georgia. This pattern accounts for 25 percent of our sample. A second trajectory has taken 16 percent of the respondents first to California and then to Georgia. A third trajectory has taken 15 percent of the group on a Mexico-Texas-Mexico-Georgia or a Mexico-Texas-Georgia course.

Most of the migrants (60 percent) born in northwest Mexico were in Mexico before changing their residence to Dalton, although many of them had previously worked elsewhere in Georgia, often with a return to Mexico prior to the resettlement in Dalton. Those from northwest Mexico do not typically pass through California or Texas before coming to Georgia; nor do they usually choose intermediate destinations. People from northeast Mexico, however, are relatively more likely to have traveled first to Texas and then to Georgia, whereas those from central and southern Mexico tend to choose California as the gateway to the United States. The central and southern Mexicans who go to Texas first also seem to choose several intermediate destinations (Florida, New York, Colorado) before settling in Dalton. This latter group is also less likely than the northerners to return to Mexico between stays in the United States, a tendency that may reflect a slower process of family reunification that results from a less prominent historical tradition of migration as compared with the central and western people. Among the central and western Mexicans, the maturation of migratory flows allows women and children to join previously unaccompanied men in coming to the United States (Massey, Goldring, and Durand 1994).

Central American migrants display one dominant trajectory: California as a first destination and then a direct move to Dalton, with few of them passing through other states. U.S.-born Latinos originate in different regions of the country and have lived in many different places (with Texas being especially prominent and California conspicuous by its relative absence) before arriving in Georgia.

Although 42.8 percent of the respondents were living in Mexico before arriving in Dalton, many of them had migrated previously to the United States on at least one occasion. Only 26 percent of all our respondents can therefore be considered inexperienced migrants (i.e., those who made Dalton their first U.S. destination). Those whose first U.S. destination was Texas or California seem to have moved very little

and came directly to Dalton from those states. By contrast, those who
went first to Florida moved around a great deal before settling in Dalton.
Those who chose Texas as a first destination also seemed to be particularly prone to return to Mexico from time to time.

REASONS FOR IMMIGRATION AND
SETTLEMENT IN DALTON

Why have Latinos decided to move to Dalton? What are the reasons
that prompted them to leave their former places of residence? The survey provides some answers to these questions. As expected, most respondents have chosen Dalton because jobs are available there.
Employment-related reasons account for two-thirds of the responses,
although other motives also figure prominently. Almost one-third of
those we interviewed offered family-related reasons (e.g., to keep the
family together) to explain their move. A related concern is the desire
of the migrants to find a better place to raise children, as compared with
big city ghetto areas.

LABOR MARKET INCORPORATION

The Dalton economy has been characterized by a more or less constant
demand for labor and a consequently low rate of unemployment. As
such, fully 94.6 percent of our male respondents and 52.4 percent of
the females are currently employed. (The remainder of the women are
engaged in household work and are not strictly speaking in the labor
market.) The carpet industry is unquestionably the most important employer of immigrant labor in Dalton: 86 percent of the men and 40 percent of the women are working in that industry. The service sector (restaurants, hotels, health facilities) employs only 3.1 percent of the men
and 3.9 percent of the women; the poultry industry provides jobs for
3.8 percent of the men and 3.1 percent of the women; education and
retail sales employ 1 percent of the men and 2.1 percent of the women.

The average hourly wage for men working in carpet manufacturing
is $8.40, which contrasts with an average of $7 per hour in the poultry
industry. Women who work in carpet plants make an average of $7.70
per hour, as compared with only $6.20 in poultry. Those few women
whose schooling and English proficiency have allowed them to find jobs

in education and banking earn an average of $9.40 per hour. Nearly half of the households earn over $20,000 per year, and nearly 10 percent of households report an annual income of more than $37,000. The rest of the group, however, lives in poverty conditions.

Although only 20 percent of the families own their own homes, fully 75 percent of the respondents told us that they intend to remain in Dalton. The immigrants feel they have arrived in Dalton to stay; they consider it a place to raise their families, not simply a location to pass through in order to earn some money.

CONCLUSIONS

Some of the factors that account for the emergence of a Latino community in Dalton are specific to that locality, while others are probably typical of the Latino diaspora in the Southeast and other new U.S. destinations. Our data clearly show that this community is fundamentally a Mexican immigrant settlement and that most of the people come from central and western Mexico, the historic center of Mexico–U.S. migration. They have arrived in Dalton with experience and knowledge about international migration, a very valuable form of migration-specific human capital (Massey and Espinosa 1997). This factor distinguishes Dalton from other new destinations where migrations have come from regions of Mexico without a lengthy tradition of U.S.-bound migration (Smith 1996).

Our analysis of migrant trajectories suggests that many of the respondents have left states of traditional Latino settlement such as California and Texas to move to Georgia. Such internal migrants are likely to be familiar with labor markets and other American institutions. Once in Dalton, however, they bring in other family members who are new to the ways of migration. Dalton is, in fact, becoming a site for the reunification and formation of families. Two indirect indicators support this conclusion: the high percentage of children of Latino origin enrolled in local public schools and the fact that half of those students were born in Latin America.

The presence of complete families in Dalton (and perhaps in other new destinations) has noteworthy consequences. The visibility of the immigrant group is certainly enhanced vis-à-vis the rest of the community. Whereas the immigration of single men has a marginal impact on the community beyond the workplace, the arrival of entire families has an effect on schools, hospitals, churches, and leisure and consumption space. The response of the host community will, however, vary depending on local economic conditions, the history of interethnic relations, and the sociopolitical context of the place. The visibility and impact of newcomers on receiving localities also depends on the size of the new destinations. In contrast with the flows that have dominated the last thirty years of immigration to the United States and that have traditionally been directed to large cities like Los Angeles, Chicago, and Houston (Waldinger 1989), recent migratory streams are also oriented toward nonmetropolitan localities like Dalton. In such smaller places, the arrival of 30,000 Latinos in a community with 100,000 inhabitants amounts to a true social and demographic revolution.

The types of labor markets in which immigrants have found employment reinforce some of these trends. First, the jobs are typical of an urban economy and provide year-round employment, thus fostering long-term and permanent moves rather than temporary or circular migration. This type of labor market incorporation also contributes to family reunification and to the development of a stable community whose members have come to stay. Second, local immigrant employment is segmented, particularly in terms of wages. For instance, jobs in poultry pay consistently less than any post in the carpet industry. In fact, immigrants use employment in poultry as an entry into the local labor market and then move on to jobs in carpet plants. Finally, the annual incomes reported in the survey exhibit an economically segmented immigrant community. Even though the Latino community in Dalton is relatively new, it already displays some economic heterogeneity.

REFERENCES

Baker, S. 1997. The "Amnesty" Aftermath: Current Policy Issues Stemming from the Legalization Programs of the 1986 Immigration Reform and Control Act. *International Migration Review* 31:5–27.

Center for Applied Research in Anthropology. 1998. *Cultural Diversity and Education: Focus on Latino Students in Georgia.* Atlanta: Georgia State University.

Durand, J. 1998. *Politica, Modelo y Patron Migratorios.* San Luis Potosí, Mexico: El Colegio de San Luis.

Durand, J., D. Massey, and F. Charvet. 1998. *The Changing Geography of Mexican Immigration to the United States: 1910–1996.* Paper presented at the Twenty-first International Congress of the Latin American Sociological Association, September 24–26, Chicago.

Gouveia, L., and R. Saenz. 1999. Latino/a Immigrants and New Social Formations in the Great Plains: An Assessment of Population Growth and Multiple Impacts. Paper presented at the 94th annual meeting of the American Sociological Association, August 6–10, Chicago.

Hamann, E. 1999. The Georgia Project: A Binational Attempt to Reinvent a School District in Response to Latino Newcomers. Ph.D. diss., University of Pennsylvania.

Hernández-León, R., and V. Zúñiga. 2000. "Making Carpet by the Mile": The Emergence of a Mexican Immigrant Community in an Industrial Region of the U.S. Historical South. *Social Science Quarterly* 81:49–66.

Hernández-León, R., V. Zúñiga, J. Shadduck, and M. Villareal. 1997. *Hispanic Community Needs Assessment.* Monterrey, Mexico: Universidad de Monterrey and the Georgia Project.

Massey, D., and K. Espinosa. 1997. What's Driving Mexico-U.S. Migration? A Theoretical, Empirical, and Policy Analysis. *American Journal of Sociology* 102:939–99.

Massey, D., L. Goldring, and J. Durand. 1994. Continuities in Transnational Migration: An Analysis of Nineteen Mexican Communities. *American Journal of Sociology* 99:1492–533.

Massey, D., R. Alarcon, J. Durand, and H. Gonzalez. 1987. *Return to Aztlan: The Social Process of International Migration from Western Mexico.* Berkeley: University of California Press.

Smith, R. 1996. Mexicans in New York: Membership and Incorporation in a New Immigrant Community. In *Latinos in New York*, ed. G. Haslip-Viera and S. Baver, 57–103. Notre Dame, Ind.: University of Notre Dame Press.

U.S. Census Bureau. 1999. *U.S. Gazetteer: 1990 Census Lookup.* http://www.census.gov/cgi-bin/gazetteer (last accessed on June 10, 2000).

Waldinger, R. 1989. Immigration and Urban Change. *Annual Review of Sociology* 15:211–32.

Contributors

Susan Andreatta is a faculty member in the Department of Anthropology at the University of North Carolina at Greensboro. Her research interests include cultural ecology, applied anthropology, and Latin America.

Carl L. Bankston is a faculty member in the Department of Sociology at Tulane University.

Colleen Blanchard is the research coordinator for the Center for Applied Research in Anthropology at Georgia State University. She specializes in reproductive health among Hispanic immigrant women.

Allan Burns is a faculty member in the Department of Anthropology at the University of Florida. He directs the Florida/Yucatan exchange program and has published widely on Maya culture and history, visual anthropology, and applied anthropology.

Jeronimo Camposeco works for Guadeloupe Social Services, assisting immigrants and refugees in South Florida. He has been an officer of Corn Maya, an organization dedicated to the rights of Guatemalan refugees.

Jack G. Dale is a student at the University of North Carolina at Greensboro.

Katherine M. Donato is currently at Rice University and formerly was a faculty member of the Department of Sociology at Louisiana State University from 1989 through 2000. Her research interests are in stratification and demography and include health, international migration, immigration policy, and the labor force activity of minority men and women in the United States.

Deborah A. Duchon is the director of the Nutrition Education for New Americans Project in the Department of Anthropology and Geography at Georgia State University. She specializes in applied research related to refugees and refugee policy, human migration, nutritional anthropology, and ethnobotany.

James D. Engstrom is affiliated with Georgia Perimeter College, Dunwoody campus.

Elizabeth Freeman is a student at the University of North Carolina at Greensboro.

Guillermo Grenier directs the Center for Labor Research and Studies at Florida International University. He is also a faculty member in the Department of Sociology and Anthropology.

David Griffith holds a joint position in the Department of Anthropology and the Institute for Coastal and Marine Resources at East Carolina University. He has been studying issues affecting working people for the past twenty years, beginning with his work among Jamaican sugar workers in Florida.

Greig Guthey is a graduate student in the Department of Geography at the University of California, Berkeley.

Rubén Hernández-León is a member of the faculty at the Universidad de Monterrey in Mexico.

Jennifer A. Hill is a research associate with the Center for Applied Research in Anthropology at Georgia State University. Her specialty is health and belief systems. She is currently working on a project involving beliefs and recovery from disasters in Mexico.

Eric C. Jones is a doctoral candidate at the University of Georgia. He is studying the effect of Ecuadorian rural-rural migration on social networks implicated in the success of agricultural cooperatives.

Ed Kissam works for Aguirre International in San Mateo, California. He conducts research on migrant education and other issues affecting farmworkers. He is currently working on a U.S. Department of Labor study of children who work in agriculture.

Kathryn A. Kozaitis is a member of the faculty of the Department of Anthropology and Geography at Georgia State University. Her research and teaching involve urban applied anthropology, global migration, relocation, and adaptation. She is currently conducting research on the cultural dimension of a systemic reform initiative in science education in the local public schools.

Arthur D. Murphy is a member of the faculty of the Department of Anthropology and Geography at Georgia State University. A social anthropologist specializing in urban households and economic development, he began research in Mexico in 1971 and has published three books and various articles on families and household adaptation to cultural and social change.

Kathleen M. Murphy is currently in the Department of Anthropology at the University of Notre Dame. She is conducting NSF-funded research in Matamoros/Brownsville concerning the experience of poverty on both sides of the border.

Laura Nieto-Studstill teaches Spanish for the Rockdale County school system of Georgia.

Martha W. Rees is a member of the faculty of Agnes Scott College in Decatur, Georgia. She is a social anthropologist specializing in household economics in Mexico and among Mexican immigrants to the United States. She has conducted research in Mexico for over fifteen years with support from the National Science Foundation and a Fulbright lectureship.

Robert E. Rhoades is a member of the faculty of the Department of Anthropology at the University of Georgia. His interest in migration stems from his studies on guest workers in Germany and their return to Turkey and Spain. He has published extensively on the role of migration in rural development and environmental impacts.

Karen Richman is affiliated with the research programs of the Department of Sociology and Anthropology at Florida International University.

Dawn T. Robinson is a faculty member in the Department of Sociology at Louisiana State University. Her current research interests include the identification of basic small-group processes.

Alex Stepick is a member of the faculty of the Department of Sociology and Anthropology at Florida International University.

John D. Studstill is a faculty member at Spelman and Morehouse Colleges.

Victor Zúñiga is a member of the faculty of the Universidad de Monterrey in Mexico.